The Grand Illusion

How the Media Used Propaganda and Dark Psychology to Elect Barack Hussein Obama

Laszlo Forseti

Black Rose Writing | Texas

First printing

ISBN: 978-1-68433-939-6
PUBLISHED BY BLACK ROSE WRITING
www.blackrosewriting.com

Printed in the United States of America
Suggested Retail Price (SRP) $19.95

The Grand Illusion is printed in Gentium Book Basic

*As a planet-friendly publisher, Black Rose Writing does its best to eliminate unnecessary waste to reduce paper usage and energy costs, while never compromising the reading experience. As a result, the final word count vs. page count may not meet common expectations.

The most brilliant propagandist technique will yield no success unless one fundamental principle is borne in mind constantly—it must confine itself to a few points and repeat them over and over.

–Joseph Goebbels, Nazi Reichsminister of Propaganda

The Grand Illusion

NOTES FROM THE AUTHORS

It is no secret the political left hates the "natural born citizen" clause in Article II, Section 1 of the U.S. Constitution. You probably heard the media and the Democrat Party at some point during the election of 2008, insisting that "natural born citizen" is not defined anywhere in the Constitution, and that Barack Obama was a natural born citizen because he was born in Hawaii.

What you really heard was propaganda. Americans may be familiar with the term but are not likely to recognize it. Americans also reject any idea of mind control techniques. That is the world of science fiction. The master of propaganda, Joseph Goebbels said, "Propaganda works best when those who are being manipulated are confident they are acting on their own free will." We will show you what propaganda is. We will show you what the Democrat Party and the media did, when they did it, and how they manipulated Americans all in an effort to elect Barack Obama.

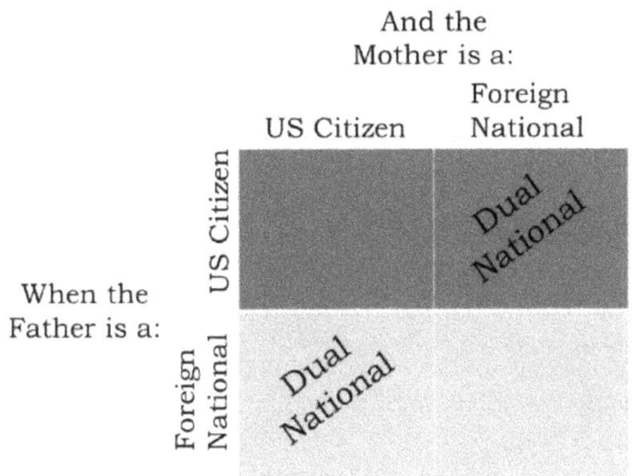

This book was made possible by many people. We, the authors of numerous articles in blogs, newspapers, law reviews, the Congressmen who repeatedly tried to amend the Constitution, and the Founding Fathers and Signers of the nation's historical documents. Authors of books, declassified references to CIA projects, military psychological operations groups, and think tanks all had a part to play in this research project. Some 234 patriots, lawyers and military men tried to stop the madness in a court of law only to be denied a hearing because of a lack of standing. There were also other people who petitioned the Federal Election Commission for relief.

Everyone cited in the book had a little story to tell. They provided the pieces to the jigsaw puzzle that were not limited to Barack Obama but included the perfidy of the Democrat Party and the mainstream media.

We collected facts and reviewed the related literature. We dumped a lot of pieces on a table and began assembling the disparate data into a coherent story. We were stunned by some of the people who were in on the plan.

Where we ended up surprised us.

What we found should shock you.

CHAPTER 1
THE HIDDEN IMPERATIVE
TO AMEND THE U.S. CONSTITUTION

One cannot begin to understand the 2008 election without being aware of the numerous attempts of members of Congress to amend the U.S. Constitution. At issue is the Constitutional requirement, truncated for clarity... "No person except a natural born citizen shall be eligible to the office of the president." There was a potential *2008* presidential candidate who (in 2003 and 2004) was positively known to be ineligible "in the eyes of the Constitution" because he wasn't a "natural born citizen." In spite of his presidential aspirations, he was ineligible under the Constitution to hold the office of the President of the United States.

Before we review our candidate's ineligibility and many of the political maneuvers that took place before, during, and after the 2004 presidential election, let's look at the players in Congress who interjected themselves into this drama solely to eliminate the "natural born citizen" requirement for president. The timing and wording of the proposed legislation coming from seemingly nowhere was odd. In politics everything has a reason for existing. In the intelligence community, there is no such thing as a coincidence.

There is only one reason these Congress members got involved: a candidate for a future election was, at that moment, *ineligible* to hold the office of the presidency simply because he wasn't a "natural born citizen." How did they know he was ineligible? Simple, the future candidate was known to be not born of U.S. citizens. These Congressmen confirmed it by their actions; their candidate was ineligible so the Constitution needed to be changed to make him an eligible and legal candidate. If any one of these Congressmen had been successful they would likely have enjoyed the perks of a new position in a presidential administration.

They were not embarking on this course of action for the benefit of all mankind but for the benefit a single person in their caucus, or who would soon be in their caucus. Most other members of Congress knew what these Congressmen and Senators were doing and their reason for doing it. It should have been a full and open process, although it was not. Those carrying the water for their chosen candidate had to be sly about what they were doing so as to escape the scrutiny of the media, the American people, and some other members of Congress. The behavior was covert so that no blame could ever be placed on the Congressmen offering the proposals. Noteworthy, these were all Democrat congressmen.

In the 245 years of the United States, there are very few recorded instances of proposed legislation to amend the Constitution to specifically remove the "natural born citizen" requirement for president and propose a much lesser standard, essentially to replace the "natural born citizen" requirement with anyone with a pulse. The Democrat's chosen future candidate was an ineligible, articulate person with a pulse and nice creases in his trousers. There is some history of the Democrat Party attempting to amend the Constitution for the benefit of one person.

In 1975, Democrat Rep. Jonathon B. Bingham [NY-22] of the 94th Congress introduced H.J.R. 33[1] which would remove the "natural born citizen" requirement for president under Article II of the U.S. Constitution. CONGRESS.GOV summarized the joint resolution: Constitutional Amendment—Provides that a citizen of the United States otherwise eligible to hold the Office of President shall not be ineligible because such citizen is not a natural born citizen. In other words, double negatives aside, *any* U.S. citizen would be eligible to be president. H.J.R. 33 was referred to the House Committee on the Judiciary but failed in committee. Maybe its failure was tied to the clumsy language of the proposal.

Undaunted, in 1977, another attempt to remove the "natural born citizen" requirement for president under Article II of the U.S. Constitution was introduced, H.J.R. 38[2] by Rep. Bingham of the 95th Congress. CONGRESS.GOV summarized: Constitutional Amendment—Permits an otherwise eligible citizen of the United States to hold the office of President even if such individual is not a natural born citizen. We admit the language was better.

For what purpose would you want to change the presidential requirements outlined in the U.S. Constitution? Here is a list of potential Democratic candidates for president in 1976:

Jimmy Carter, former governor of Georgia
Morris Udall, U.S. Representative from Arizona
Jerry Brown, Governor of California
George Wallace, Governor of Alabama
Ellen McCormack, was born in The Bronx to Irish immigrants
Frank Church, U.S. Senator from Idaho
Henry M. Jackson, U.S. Senator from Washington, mother and father were both immigrants from Norway
Fred R. Harris, former U.S. Senator from Oklahoma
Robert Byrd, U.S. Senator from West Virginia
Milton Shapp, Governor of Pennsylvania, mother and father were both Jewish
Sargent Shriver, former U.S. Ambassador to France, from Maryland, was of partial German ancestry. Married Eunice Kennedy, the third daughter of Joseph Kennedy Sr. and Rose Kennedy
Birch Bayh, U.S. Senator from Indiana
Lloyd Bentsen, U.S. Senator from Texas
Terry Sanford, former governor of North Carolina
Walter Fauntroy, U.S. Delegate from Washington, D.C.

There was no ambiguity in the language of Rep. Bingham's proposal—the proposed amendment from the Democrat would "make eligible" a person who is not a "natural born citizen." There is little doubt who the amendment would benefit directly, Robert Sargent Shriver, Junior the suave and urbane diplomat, the war hero and husband of Eunice Kennedy, the daughter of Joseph Kennedy, Sr. and Rose Kennedy. The only person on the list of presidential candidates who was not a natural born citizen was Sargent Shriver. Shriver had a pedigree and was a descendant of David Shriver, who signed the Maryland Constitution and Bill of Rights at Maryland's Constitutional Convention of 1776.

By a cursory glance of his birth certificate, one would not immediately know that Sargent Shriver was not born of two U.S. citizens. Only after a little more digging into the history of his parents does one find Sargent Shriver's mother was of German ancestry and was not a naturalized U.S. citizen before Sargent Shriver's birth. It didn't work out for Representative Bingham or for Sargent Shriver. Article II of the U.S. Constitution was not amended.

Twenty-five years later, Democrat members of Congress began their own efforts to eliminate the "natural born citizen" requirement for president. They had an ineligible candidate too. The Democrats had a candidate who could not meet the "natural born citizen" requirement for president. There was one person in particular. Who was it? That was a Democrat Party secret of the first order.

On June 11, 2003 Democrat Rep. Vic Snyder [AR-2] of the 108th Congress introduced H.J.R 59[3] which would remove the "natural born citizen" requirement for president under Article II of the U.S. Constitution. CONGRESS.GOV summarized the joint resolution: Constitutional Amendment—Makes a person who has been a citizen of the United States for at least 35 years and who has been a resident within the United States for at least 14 years eligible to hold the office of President or Vice President.

Unlike Rep. Bingham's H.J.Rs which received no co-sponsors, Rep. Snyder welcomed the following co-sponsors: Rep. John Conyers, Jr., [MI-14]; Rep. William D. Delahunt, [MA-10]; Rep. Barney Frank, [MA-4]; Rep. Darrell E. Issa, [CA-49]; Rep. Ray LaHood, [IL-18]; and Rep. Christopher Shays, [CT-4].

On September 3, 2003, Rep. John Conyers, Jr. [MI-14] introduced H.J.R. 67[4]. CONGRESS.GOV summarized the joint resolution: Constitutional Amendment—Makes a person who has been a citizen of the United States for at least 20 years eligible to hold the office of President. Co-sponsor: Rep. Brad Sherman, [CA-27].

Republicans in Congress took note of the Democrat's machinations to amend the Constitution and fought back with their own proposed legislation. Noteworthy, these actions *weren't* reported in the newspapers and they *weren't* carried live on the cable news channels.

On February 25, 2004, Republican Senator Don Nickles [OK] of the 108th Congress introduced S.2128[5]. CONGRESS.GOV summarized the proposed legislation: Natural Born Citizen Act—Defines the constitutional term "natural born citizen," to establish eligibility for the Office of President, as: (1) any person born in, and subject to the jurisdiction of, the United States; and (2) any person born outside the United States who derives citizenship at birth from U.S. citizen parents, or who is adopted by the age of 18 by U.S. citizen parents who are otherwise eligible to transmit citizenship. Co-sponsors included Sen. James M. Inhofe, [OK] and Sen. Mary L. Landrieu, [LA].

The key phrase of this proposed legislation was, "...any person born outside the United States who derives citizenship at birth from U.S. citizen parents." The essential element was that the "natural born citizen" clause remained fully intact from its initial rendering and its definition was updated to include adopted children. Also note, the Republican Senator did not try to turn the U.S. Constitution into a dictionary. Corrections or updated qualifications are done through legislation; in this case children adopted by U.S. citizens are also to be considered "natural born citizens."

On September 15, 2004, Republican Rep. Dana Rohrabacher [CA-46] of the 108th Congress introduced H.J.R. 104[6]. CONGRESS.GOV summarized the joint resolution: Constitutional Amendment—Makes eligible for the Office of the President non-native born persons who have held U.S. citizenship for at least 20 years and who are otherwise eligible to hold such Office. No co-sponsors.

On January 4, 2005, Rep. John Conyers, Jr. introduced H.J.R. 2[7] to the 109th Congress. CONGRESS.GOV summarized the joint resolution: Constitutional Amendment—Makes a person who has been a citizen of the United States for at least 20 years eligible to hold the Office of President. Co-sponsor: Rep. Brad Sherman, [CA-27].

On February 1, 2005, Rep. Dana Rohrabacher [CA-46] tried again, H.J.R. 15[8] which proposed an amendment to the Constitution of the United States to make eligible for the Office of President a person who is not a "natural born citizen" of the United States but has been a United States citizen for at least 20 years. No co-sponsors.

There was no ambiguity in the language or the timing of the proposed amendments from the Republican Congressman from California that would "make eligible" a person who is not a "natural born citizen." Rep. Dana Rohrabacher's amendment would benefit California Governor Arnold Schwarzenegger. There were open campaigns and petitions in California to amend the Constitution just so the Austrian-born governor of Austrian parents could run for President of the United States.

On April 14, 2005, Rep. Vic Snyder [AR-2] tried again with H.J.R. 42[9]. Like Rep. Rohrabacher's proposed amendment, Rep. Snyder proposed an amendment to the Constitution of the United States that would permit persons who are not "natural born citizens" of the United States, but who have been citizens of the United States for at least 35 years, to be eligible to hold the offices of President and Vice President. CONGRESS.GOV summarized the joint resolution: Constitutional Amendment—Makes a person who has been a citizen of the United States for at least 35 years and who has been a resident within the United States for at least 14 years eligible to hold the office of President or Vice President. Co-Sponsor Rep. Christopher Shays, [CT-4].

Again, there is no ambiguity in the language—the proposed amendment from a Democrat would "make eligible" a person who is not a "natural born citizen," but who had been a citizen of the U.S. for at least 35 years and had been a resident within the U.S. for at least 14 years. And there is no ambiguity about whom the amendment would directly and specifically benefit. The proposed legislation would benefit keynote speaker of the 2004 Democratic National Convention whose speech electrified the FleetCenter in Boston, Massachusetts, Illinois State Senator Barack Obama II. In his speech he mentioned the title of his upcoming book and regaled the dreams from his father and grandfather. Overnight, Barack Obama was introduced to all of America and became a national figure. Immediately after the Democratic National Convention there were discussions of Senator Barack Obama running for president on radio and network shows from coast to coast.

In all of the proposed legislation there was nary a written comment that "natural born citizen" was not defined in the U.S. Constitution. Congressmen taking the podium verbally indicated this deficiency and the proposed legislation was to correct that omission.

Was this true?

No. What was proposed wasn't to correct a faulty Constitution, but to amend the Constitution for the benefit of a single person in the U.S. population who happened to be ineligible for the office of the president.

Senator Barack Obama II did his part to announce his presidential aspirations—his book *Dreams from My Father*—was published in August 2004. The Democrats who introduced amendments to the Constitution of the United States that would allow persons who were not "natural born citizens" of the United States to be eligible to hold the office of President realized they had a major problem as early as 2003 (as *Dreams from My Father* was being written) and in 2004 (when *Dreams from My Father* was finally published). At that time, a Republican, Dennis Hastert, was the Speaker of the House. Republican *and* Democrat Party efforts to amend the U.S. Constitution failed in committee.

On February 28, 2008, Democrat Senator Claire McCaskill, [MO] tried a backdoor approach that would allow persons who were not "natural born citizens" of the United States to be eligible to hold the office of president as an attachment to a military bill in S.2678[10]. CONGRESS.GOV summarized the senate bill: Children of Military Families Natural Born Citizen Act—Declares that the term "natural born Citizen" in Article II, Section 1, Clause 5 of the Constitution, dealing with the criteria for election to President of the United States, includes any person born to any U.S. citizen while serving in the active or reserve components of the U.S. armed forces. Noteworthy co-sponsors included presidential candidate Sen. Hillary Rodham Clinton, [NY]; presidential candidate Sen Barack Obama II, [IL]; Sen Robert Menendez, [NJ]; and Sen Tom Coburn, [OK]. All Democrats.

Had S.2678 been passed, it was just a hop, skip, and a jump to go from "any person born to any U.S. citizen while serving in the active or reserve components of the U.S. armed forces" to "any person born to any U.S. citizen." Under the implication that the Constitution somehow disqualified the children of members of the armed services (as an example, if these children were born abroad), the legislation would ensure some fix to a problem that did not exist. This was true sleight of hand, *prestidigitation*; those were the magic words the Democrat Party had always sought for their chosen candidate—*any person born to any U.S. citizen*—not the two-century old *standard* of a *person born to U.S. citizens, plural.* These people knew what they were doing and how to manipulate, how to create diversionary legislation all so an ineligible candidate could become eligible.

S.2678 was the Democrat senator's response to Republican Senator Don Nickles' S.2128, the Natural Born Citizen Act. Democrat Senator Claire McCaskill famously endorsed Senator Obama in 2008 instead of Senator Hillary Clinton and her Senate bill is also an example of how Democrats worked to undermine the U.S. Constitution to benefit a single Democrat. We will see more work from former Senator McCaskill in a later chapter.

In summary, for over two centuries there had not been a single legitimate effort to eliminate the "natural born citizen" requirement for president under Article II, Section 1 of the U.S. Constitution. The mold was shattered in 1975 and 1977 when Democrat Rep. Bingham of New York proposed amendments to the Constitution which would have made eligible the most likely and only candidate for president who wasn't a "natural born citizen," Sargent Shriver, a war hero and a former U.S. Ambassador.

The attempts to amend the U.S. Constitution and eliminate the "natural born citizen" requirement for president under Article II were spurting out of Congressional offices as if from a firehose.

J.B. Williams of NewsWithViews.com and others found that there had been "no less than eight attempts[11] in twenty-two months" where Democrat members of Congress introduced House Joint Resolutions to eliminate the "natural born citizen" requirement for president.

Republicans knew that the Democrats were trying to amend the Constitution for one of their future presidential candidates. They responded with a counter amendment that reemphasized or clarified the meaning of "natural born citizen" as children born of *U.S. citizens*, not a *single citizen*, and would include the adopted children of U.S. citizens.

A sports term, "Pound the Rock," is all about having the ability and the will to keep plugging away at adversity, to keep hitting until the rock cracks. It is a relentlessness and a willingness to sacrifice everything for the team, knowing that the very next hit could be the one that breaks the rock. During the run-up to the 2008 election we saw how the Democrats relentlessly attacked the rock, the "natural born citizen" clause. Each one of those proposed pieces of legislation was designed crack the rock, create a fissure in the U.S. Constitution. It is a classic case of the BIG LIE in propaganda practices. The hammer in all of these efforts was the BIG LIE, that "natural born citizen" was not defined in the U.S. Constitution.

The Big Lie is a major untruth uttered frequently by leaders as a means of duping and controlling the constituency.

Adolph Hitler

For Senator Obama, Democrat Senators and Congressmen lined up in droves, pulled out all the stops, and repeated the refrain that "natural born citizen" is not defined anywhere in the Constitution. They proposed legislation to change the "natural born citizen" *standard* of "children born to U.S. citizens" to anyone born to a single U.S. citizen so that their chosen candidate had a legitimate shot as a legal and *eligible* candidate for the presidency. These people did everything they could do to advance the BIG LIE within the letter of the law. And all along the way Democrats hid their actions like common criminals hiding a purloined copy of *Playboy* under their coat. Republicans were transparent and had "Amend for Arnold" campaigns throughout California. Democrats kept their cards close to their chest as they kept pounding the rock while the media ensured no one would ever notice.

Not every item of news should be published. Rather must those who control news policies endeavor to make every item of news serve a certain purpose.

Joseph Goebbels

These are the actions of politicians; these could have been called "political favors," which is another term that is not defined in the U.S. Constitution.

CHAPTER 2
THE NATURAL BORN CITIZEN CLAUSE

In an article entitled, "The *Washington Post* Confessed to a very Big Lie," author Andrea Widburg of American Thinker provided the *details*[1] of the "BIG LIE," but also faced the reality of the situation with "...this is par for the course for the modern Pravda media. Second, as long as there are no consequences, and *there never are*, it's irrelevant that the *Washington Post* behaved in a morally corrupt, fraudulent way." Her conclusion was the journalistic equivalent of Mad magazine's Alfred E. Newman saying, "What, Me worry? I can say or do anything I want."

Our mass media are not what the Founders envisioned when they crafted the First Amendment. Today's mass media are not the Fourth Estate in the classical sense, but they have become a Fifth Column, defined as any group of people who undermine a larger group from within, usually in favor of an enemy group or nation. There should not be any question, a Fifth Column media only serves to help Democrats and undermine Republicans. Americans may assume the media is fair and balanced, but the media chose sides long ago.

As we have seen, from 2003 through 2008 the mainstream media barely provided any coverage on the attempts of Congress to eliminate the "natural born citizen[2]" clause in the U.S. Constitution. There were some in the Republican Party who saw the White House in Arnold Schwarzenegger's future; they took to the airwaves and the Internet in an effort to generate support for a Constitutional amendment to make Schwarzenegger's run possible. There were articles which promoted an "Amend for Arnold[3]" campaign; there were fundraisers, websites, radio ads and television specials to promote changing the U.S. Constitution so California's Republican governor could run for president.

Arnold was a bodybuilder and a movie star who played U.S. heroes. The California media claimed there was "surprising support" from people across the nation. But there was more evidence that Americans viewed an

"Amend for Arnold" campaign as somewhat dishonest. There was little support to amend the Constitution under any pretext that would benefit an ineligible candidate.

Since 2008, the American media have become worse than the old Soviet Union's *Pravda*. The Russian painter, Elena Gorokhova, expressed what all Russians knew about their state-run mass media:

The rules are simple: they lie to us, we know they're lying, they know we know they're lying, but they keep lying to us, and we keep pretending to believe them.

The Russian people knew they were being lied to every day, Americans are largely clueless or indifferent. Many Americans refuse to believe, do not know, or do not care if they are being lied to by their media as long as the sports scores are correct.

Americans discovering that the media use propaganda in their reporting could be Orwellian and is not to be believed. As this book was being written, two headlines came across the wire, "CNN Director Admits Network Ran 'Propaganda' to get Trump 'Voted Out[4],'" and "Is it really possible that the cable news networks have deep ties to the Democrats?[5]"

Few believe the media actually use propaganda, behavior modification, and mind control techniques in certain situations to manipulate unsuspecting Americans. We will show when and how they did it. Let's review a few statements of law and facts—they are available for review in the archival record. Let's see how the media responded to these.

The mass media grotesquely interfered with the election of 2008 regarding Barack Obama's eligibility to be the President of the United States. At the heart of this issue of eligibility is what "natural born citizen" means. Republicans take the Constitutional view that "natural born citizen" is a political *standard*, a not-to-be-negotiated requirement for the office of the President. Democrats would love to do away with it once and for all.

From President George Washington to President George W. Bush, from 1789 to 2009, all presidents fulfilled the requirements to hold the Office of the President. Here are the specific, absolute, and unequivocal requirements of the U.S. Constitution, Article II, Section 1[6]:

No person except a natural born citizen, or a citizen of the United States, at the time of the adoption of this Constitution, shall be eligible to the office of

President; neither shall any person be eligible to that office who shall not have attained to the age of thirty five years, and been fourteen Years a resident within the United States.[2]

To Republicans, this is the Constitution; this is proof. To Democrats, this is only *evidence*, like a blood stain that suggests a crime may have been committed. There may be other interpretations. For Republicans the Constitution is very emphatic when it states *No person except a natural born citizen* meets the requirements to be president. For the Democrats and the media, they believe there is *evidence* that the Constitution is likely faulty or that it is vague when referencing this most basic presidential eligibility requirement.

Television and newspaper announcements, Hollywood surrogates, television shows such as *The View*, *The Ellen DeGeneres Show*, *The Tonight Show*, *Oprah!* and others ignored the Constitutional *standard* while the media continually repeated their manufactured *hearsay evidence* that the "natural born citizen" clause "isn't defined anywhere in the Constitution," that its meaning in the Constitution is "vague and arbitrary." Democrats have argued and tried to provide more *evidence* to buttress their case with an argument that the U.S. Constitution was simply "a relic of Eighteenth-Century concerns that have little relevance to modern America[7]." This argument is a Democrat talking point; it is not factual, it is clearly *hearsay*. It is an opinion used to support a lie. The BIG LIE in propaganda.

If the Democrat Party brought a case to the U.S. Supreme Court and insisted that "native-born citizens" should be used instead of "natural born citizen," for whatever reason, the Supreme Court Justices would have to say "native-born citizens" is Unconstitutional. The Constitution says "natural born citizen." These comments and others were not taken to the U.S. Supreme Court to determine if the Democrat Party's version of things were Constitutional but were repeated in left-wing newspapers and networks thousands of times a day all across America.

A lie told once remains a lie but a lie told a thousand times becomes the truth.

Joseph Goebbels

One political party tried to foist their argument as *evidence* onto the U.S. body politic that the Constitution is "a relic of Eighteenth-Century concerns that have little relevance to modern America." This opinion may or may not be so, but it is totally irrelevant. They have used this line as an *insinuation*, a *dark psy*chology tool called a "trial balloon" to inject confusion. They were trying to create *evidence* with political words to attack the integrity of the Constitution and to redefine what is Constitutional. Their interpretation is an *opinion*, bogus manufactured *evidence* presented as fact, and the true meaning of their concept is obfuscated by flowery words and repetition.

The assertion that "natural born citizen" isn't defined anywhere in the Constitution was extensively repeated in the public domain despite the fact that "natural born citizen" is in the Constitution and is therefore *Constitutional*. For propaganda to work there must be repetition. The Democrat Party and the mass media complex did whatever was necessary to ignore the Constitution and keep their version of manufactured *evidence* at the forefront of an audience of thousands to create the illusion that their ineligible candidate was Constitutionally eligible for the presidency. This is *The Grand Illusion*.

The Founders relied heavily on the work of Swiss philosopher Emerich de Vattel and his 1758 legal treatise, *The Law of Nations*[8] when drafting the U.S. Constitution. In *The Law of Nations*, in Book One, Chapter 19, in the section titled "Of the citizens and natives," de Vattel defined the term "natural born citizen" as:

"*...The natives, or natural-born citizens, are those born in the country, of parents who are citizens... The country of the fathers is therefore that of the children; and these become true citizens merely by their tacit consent. I say that, in order to be of the country, it is necessary that a person be born of a father who is a citizen; for, if he is born there of a foreigner, it will be only the place of his birth, and not his country.*"

The term "natural born citizen" was widely known and used by our forefathers. It was a normal term of usage like the Second Amendment's to keep and bear arms as in the *Right to keep and bear arms shall not be infringed*, another shocking display of a term not defined in the U.S. Constitution.

The American Congress' first act concerning citizenship and who qualified as a "natural born citizen" was the *Naturalization Act of 1790*[9]. It stated unambiguously that "*...the children of citizens of the United States,* that may be born beyond the sea or out of the limits of the United States, *shall be considered as natural born citizens.*" (Act of March 26, 1790. 1 Stat. pages 103, 104 [emphasis added]). Please note the words *shall be considered.* The definition of "natural born citizen" is directive by word of law and not negotiable. It is a *standard.* "Natural born citizen" means only one thing: *the children of citizens of the United States.* Period.

There it is, the actual definition of "natural born citizen," codified in law. Act, chapter, page numbers. How simple is that? The children of citizens of the United States. A child can be born abroad or north and south of the thirteen colonies—it doesn't matter. As long as the child is born of U.S. citizens, then that child is in the special category of "natural born citizen" and eligible to be President of the United States.

This *is* a little different from de Vattel's definition in *The Law of Nations.* Let's review de Vattel and what he said in 1758, "*...The natives, or natural-born citizens, are those born in the country, of parents who are citizens... The country of the fathers is therefore that of the children; and these become true citizens merely by their tacit consent. I say that, in order to be of the country, it is necessary that a person be born of a father who is a citizen; for, if he is born there of a foreigner, it will be only the place of his birth, and not his country.*"

So...The natives are those born in the country. Natural-born citizens are those born of parents who are citizens...wherever they reside.... Natural-born citizens can be native born but being native-born doesn't necessarily mean you are born of parents who are citizens.

Here is the brilliance of Alexander Hamilton. He solved the question of "natural born citizen" during the time when it was the custom for men to dominate politics and the political landscape. Instead of using de Vattel's version verbatim of what constitutes a "natural born citizen" "*...it is necessary that a person be born of a father who is a citizen,*" Hamilton's version included second-class citizens who didn't even have the right to vote, "*...it is necessary that a person be born of United States citizens...*" By elevating American *women,* American *mothers* as citizens, Hamilton's genius created the *standard* for future candidates for the presidency of the United States.

With incredible insight Hamilton saw that, "*...those born of parents who are citizens will always be natural-born citizens" and that natives may not be citizens at all.* In the first law on citizenship, Congress considered the ratiocination of twenty Founders: Children *born of U.S.* citizens are *natural-born citizens.* Those that suggested only "native-born citizens" should be eligible to be president showed an incredible lack of understanding of what the term could mean.

Anyone with a computer and a search engine can find our nation's first naturalization law and see that this definition on pages 103 and 104 of that document is not vague or arbitrary; the "natural born citizen" clause in the U.S. Constitution is quite specific and actually comports with de Vattel's treatise, *The Law of Nations*. The difference was that Hamilton ignored the male prerogatives of children born to men and used persons born to citizens.

What made the office of the U.S. President exclusive was by placing emphasis not on where a child was born but to whom. Citizens, plural, of America. To this day, many other countries of the world subscribe to de Vattel's version of presidential candidates as "*...a person born of a father who is a citizen*" and do not recognize the contributions of the mother. Hamilton was very progressive.

Note: Centuries after his death it was found that President George Washington had a number of overdue library books dating back over two centuries. One of them was de Vattel's *The Law of Nations*. Why are we not surprised?

Contrary to the leftist fact-checking organization Snopes and the mainstream media, the term "natural born citizen" *was* in widespread use in the colonies at the time of the Revolutionary War. After the *Declaration of Independence* had been sent across the Atlantic to King George III, Americans of the 13 colonies began the daunting task of creating a government "by the people, for the people." The 13 colonies would become states. The 13 states would have a *president*, not a king. No longer would the people of the 13 colonies be considered *subjects of the Crown;* Americans would become *citizens of the United States*. When someone asked, "Just what are the requirements going to be for this president? *Our president!*" Alexander Hamilton and twenty Founders had an answer: Derived from de Vattel's *The Law of Nations* anyone born of parents who were citizens of the United States would be the only ones eligible to become president. Hamilton ensured presidential requirements were put into the U.S. Constitution; Congress can change a law with a voice vote, but to amend the Constitution to change the presidential requirements would require more work.

The colonists were fighting England in 1775. The *Declaration of Independence* was signed on the Fourth of July, 1776. The U.S. Constitution was signed on September 17, 1787. It took 12 years *of war* for the colonialists to move from being classified as subjects to citizens. United States citizens. During this time our Founders engaged in a deliberate process.

While the 13 colonies were at war with England fighting for their lives and freedom, the signers of the *Declaration of Independence* and the Founders drafted and wrote the U.S. Constitution, the *Bill of Rights*, and established the laws of the land, such as the first *Naturalization Act*. To expedite the process, the Founders used *The Law of Nations* as a reference, for efficiency, economy, and effectiveness. They unabashedly used concepts in *the Law of Nature* to write the U.S. Constitution and U.S. laws.

Our first Americans used the word "citizen" from ancient Greece. Citizenship wasn't simply an ancient concept; it arose from an appreciation of the importance of freedom. The Founders arranged their political institutions, not to establish an empire, but to be and remain free men. These were the actions of thinking men trying to build a nation, not criminals trying to steal one.

To fully understand the significance of the rest of the Constitutional phrase, defining eligibility for president, "*or a Citizen of the United States, at the time of the Adoption of this Constitution...*," it is necessary to recognize three significant dates:

1. July 4, 1776, the date on which the Declaration of Independence was signed making the residents of the thirteen colonies citizens of the United States.
2. June 21, 1788, the date on which ratification by the State of New Hampshire made the Constitution the official law of the land.

3. July 4, 1811, the date after which the first "natural born" citizens... those born to U.S. citizens *after* July 4, 1776... became 35 years of age.

The Constitution requires that in addition to being a "natural born citizen" and a resident of the United States for at least fourteen years, those who would seek the presidency must be at least thirty-five years of age. However, the only "natural born citizens" available on June 21, 1788, the day the Constitution was ratified, were children under twelve years of age. To solve that problem, the Framers added a grandfather clause. This made it possible for newly-minted U.S. citizens... all U.S. residents for at least fourteen years and all at least thirty-five years of age, but none "natural born" as they were born to parents who were British subjects prior to July 4, 1776... to lead the nation. This was necessary until such time as a body of individuals born to U.S. citizen parents *after* the Declaration of Independence reached age thirty-five.

For example, our first seven presidents... George Washington, John Adams, Thomas Jefferson, James Madison, James Monroe, John Quincy Adams, and Andrew Jackson... were over 35 years old and U.S. citizens because they were born in what later became the United States of America, but they were not "natural born citizens" because their parents may have been British subjects at the time they were born. Martin Van Buren, our eighth president, was born at Kinderhook, New York on December 5, 1782, six years and five months *after* the Declaration of Independence. Unlike his seven predecessors, he was not just a U.S. citizen, he was a "natural born" citizen... the first president, at least thirty-five years of age, who was born to U.S. citizen parents *after* July 4, 1776. Here we begin to appreciate the brilliance of the Founding Fathers and to understand the concept of American *allegiance.*

In addition to the *Declaration of Independence* several other documents outlined the specific grievances the signers and the Founders had with the British King George III. Looking closely, we see many of these complaints being identified, codified, and rectified in our *Bill of Rights.*

From the *Declaration of Independence*, the complaint: *For quartering large bodies of armed troops among us.* The *Third Amendment* was written to read: No soldier shall, in time of peace be quartered in any house, without the consent of the owner, nor in time of war, but in a manner to be prescribed by law. The *Third Amendment* prevents government from forcing homeowners to allow soldiers to use their homes. Before the Revolutionary War, British laws gave British soldiers the right to take over private homes.

From the *Declaration of Independence,* the complaint: *He has combined with others to subject us to a jurisdiction foreign to our constitution, and unacknowledged by our laws; giving his Assent to their Acts of pretended Legislation.* The *Fourth Amendment* states that, "The right of the people to be secure in their persons, houses, papers, and effects, against unreasonable searches and seizures, shall not be violated, and no warrants shall issue, but upon probable cause, supported by oath or affirmation, and particularly describing the place to be searched, and the persons or things to be seized." The *Fourth Amendment* bars the government from unreasonable search and seizure of an individual or their private property. The King gave his consent for acts of pretended legislation. The *Fourth Amendment* declares the authorities cannot make up charges against citizens.

From the *Declaration of Independence,* the complaint: *For protecting them, by a mock Trial, from punishment for any Murders which they should commit on the Inhabitants of these States. For cutting off our Trade with all parts of the world, For imposing Taxes on us without our Consent, For depriving us in many cases, of the benefits of Trial by Jury, For transporting us beyond Seas to be tried for pretended offences.* The *Fifth Amendment*: No person shall be held to answer for a capital, or otherwise infamous crime, unless on a presentment or indictment of a grand jury, except in cases arising in the land or naval forces, or in the militia, when in actual service in time of war or public danger; nor shall any person be subject for the same offense to be twice put in jeopardy of life or limb; nor shall be compelled in any criminal case to be a witness against himself, nor be deprived of life, liberty, or property, without due process of law; nor shall private property be taken for public use, without just compensation.

The *Fifth Amendment* provides several protections for people accused of crimes. It states that serious criminal charges must be started by a grand jury. A person cannot be tried twice for the same offense (double jeopardy) or have property taken away without just compensation.

Americans have the right against self-incrimination and cannot be imprisoned without due process of law (fair procedures and trials.)

Review the *Declaration of Independence*. It is a much more thorough and complex document than our instructors led us to believe in school. Our Founders first identified their complaints with the King through the *Declaration of Independence*, then sought to resolve those complaints for Americans with a *Bill of Rights*.

There is a backstory for some of the decisions the Founders made when considering input from colonialists and drafting the Constitution and its laws. Many of those backstories were the letters between the signers of the *Declaration of Independence* and the Founders who were dedicated to creating the new country. These documents are recorded for posterity and are found in *The Records of the Federal Convention of 1787*[10] and the *Federalist Papers. The Records of the Federal Convention of 1787* is like the email correspondence from the Founders and provided by an open-source Freedom of Information Act request. These men, crafting the language of legislation, were not prone to the vague or arbitrary but used precise words.

In Alexander Hamilton's writings, a few of the Founding Fathers sought more exclusivity for the office of the presidency. They held the belief that the U.S. Constitution should have included the additional phraseology of "native-born citizen" to give more exclusivity for a requirement for president. Throughout *The Records of the Federal Convention of 1787* there are multiple instances in which the terms "native-born citizen" and "natural born citizen" are used in discussions on the requirements for the future president, but during the writing of the U.S. Constitution, "natural born citizen" won out and has a special place in the history of America. It has a specific meaning and was forever codified in the *Naturalization Act of 1790* as our Founding documents were being drafted. It is elegant and simple—a child born of citizens of the United States of America is a natural born citizen of the United States of America. And any deviation to this Constitutional requirement for President of the United States would be unconstitutional.

Americans fought and died for America. We have illegal immigrants crossing our border every day, some of which are pregnant. Why would simply being born in the country be sufficient qualifications to become president?

Constitutional scholars have always had the proof at their disposal (de Vattel's 1758 *The Law of Nations* and *The Records of the Federal Convention of 1787*) to show that the term "natural born citizen" predates its *inclusion* in the 1787 U.S. Constitution. To get the full effect of a letter from one of the Founding Fathers and the future first Chief Justice of the Supreme Court John Jay wrote to General George Washington[11] it must be put into context. Recall from the *Declaration of Independence* the complaint of the King of England: *He has affected to render the Military independent of and superior to the Civil power.* The Founders believed this situation—having a military independent of and superior to the civil power—was illegal and could not exist in a free America. There was much discussion on the topic. Now John Jay's letter:

Permit me to hint, whether it would not be wise...to provide a strong check to the admission of Foreigners into the administration of our national Government, and to declare expressly that the command in chief of the american (sic) army shall not be given to, nor devolve on, any but a natural born citizen.

John Jay, thinking aloud to his friend, that it probably wasn't a great idea to have foreigners in the government, that there should be "*...a strong check to the admission of Foreigners into the administration of our national Government.*"

So, before the Founders put pen to paper with signatures and votes, Jay and Washington agreed: under no circumstances would there be foreigners in the national Government's administration, that the military is not to lord over civilians but to be subordinate to civilian leaders, and the commander in chief would be a "natural born citizen, the civilian President of the United States."

These are damning pieces of evidence which refute every aspect of the Democrat Party's tortuous, disingenuous, and unconstitutional platform that "natural born citizen" isn't defined anywhere in the Constitution, or is vague or arbitrary, or whatever excuse pops up when they shake their Magic 8 Ball. Their propaganda cannot stand up to the scrutiny of facts and truth. "Natural born citizen" is constitutional; anything else short of amending the Constitution is unconstitutional.

Starting at ground zero, with the birth of a nation, with the *Declaration of Independence,* the Founder's had to draft wording to define the requirements for their new president. The Founder's stated intent, captured in The *Federalist Papers* and in letters in *The Records of the Federal Convention of 1787,* was to consider and design presidential eligibility requirements on the basis of *total allegiance to America.* Their intent disallows the 2008 *specious red herring argument* over where a child was born and is summarized in The *Federalist Papers*: No. 68[12], *The Mode of Electing the President.* Alexander Hamilton expressed his concerns of preventing *foreigners*, who would have allegiance to their home country, from gaining the top position in the administration of the national government. A child born in America who was a citizen of two countries could be brought up to have allegiance not to America but to a foreign power. Hamilton wrote:

Nothing was more to be desired than that every practicable obstacle should be opposed to cabal, intrigue, and corruption. These most deadly adversaries of republican government might naturally have been expected to make their approaches from more than one quarter, but chiefly from the desire in foreign powers to gain an improper ascendant in our councils. How could they better gratify this, than by raising a creature of their own to the chief magistracy of the Union?

You have one country and fight for it, I have two and have to choose for one and against the other.

Cesar Romero as
Captain Nicholas Niesterstein
Rendezvous (1935)

Many of the letters contained in *The Records of the Federal Convention of* 1787 demonstrated their concerns of *foreigners* anywhere in the new government. King George III didn't send all of his front-line army to roust the revolutionaries; he threw foreigners and mercenaries who were little more than contract criminals at the colonies for various reasons. They were to fight, rape, pillage, and plunder, to create turmoil, and *infiltrate* the fledging government for the purposes of conquering it.

The letters in *The Records of the Federal Convention of* 1787 reflected that, for the colonists, it was an imperative issue of *allegiance* then and should have been an issue of allegiance in 2008. But the Democrats of today have severe allegiance issues. The Democrats of today may claim they are patriots, but it is their definition or their version of *patriots*. That they are patriots is propaganda, another BIG LIE. If they are not burning the flag, then they're standing on it or dragging it through the mud. Not all, but there are a sufficient number of Democrats who are vociferous opposition soldiers who work as clandestine anarchists to undermine the nation.

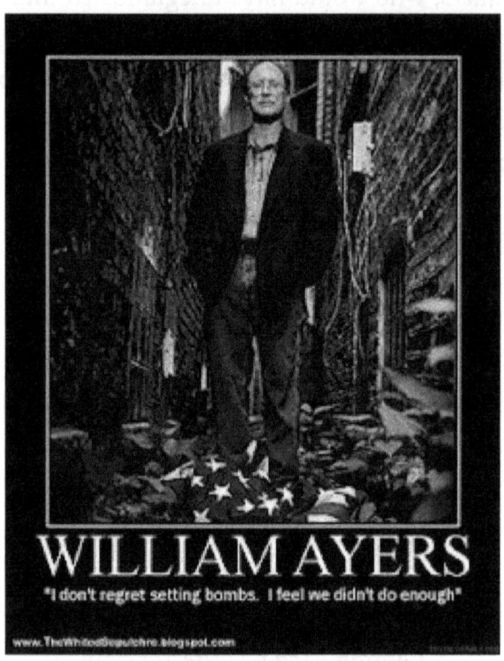

Domestic terrorist and Weather Underground leader,
Bill Ayers, standing on the U.S. Flag

In 1787, it was the King's agenda to dismantle the rebellious colonies' scheme of independence. In 2008, it was beginning to look as if the Democrat Party's agenda to dismantle the Constitution was well underway as they ran an obviously ineligible candidate for president while the media flooded their outlets with the silent weapons of propaganda, such as censorship and diversion. The media had a moratorium on never using Barack Obama's middle name. The goal was to keep the adult population attention diverted away from the candidate's presumed religion if his middle name was used. When John McCain was asked if it was appropriate to use Senator Obama's middle name, McCain said, "No, it is not. Any comment that is disparaging of either Senator Clinton or Senator Obama is totally inappropriate."[13]

The Democrats' brand of patriotism was never more evident than at the opening of their national conventions in 2000, 2004, 2008 and so on. They had no American Flags on the dais or anywhere in the convention hall when the cameras were turned on. They gave it no thought until it was pointed out that, "...ummm, why don't you have any flags in here?" We suppose in the Democrat vernacular, patriotism means never bringing an American Flag to a presidential convention unless forced to.

The Democrats today hide behind the flag as if were tri-colored camouflage. The BIG LIE is that they love and respect the American Flag but the truth is demonstrated when there are no flags on the stage, or the flags come out only for show, or when it is imperative to deflect their obvious lack of patriotism. These are patriots of another army as articulated in the Oath of Office as *domestic enemies*. The Democrats today don't say the Pledge of Allegiance and visibly recoil from any suggestion that they should. For all practical purposes, they have excised the Pledge of Allegiance from the Democrat Party charter, and they have had some success in state legislatures removing the Pledge from schools. All of the "missing flag drama" at the 2008 DNC was anathema to half of the Americans watching at home. The other half might have been treated to a glowing background story that served as nothing more than propaganda, that their candidate for president had never been taught the words to the Pledge of Allegiance and didn't know the National Anthem because he had been living in Indonesia attending a Muslim *madrassa* during his formative years. In other words, he was a victim of his upbringing and it would be irresponsible to hold him accountable for not knowing these most basic American customs.

Candidate Obama was caught standing with his hands folded in front of him instead of covering his heart during a rendition of the National Anthem. The video left the impression that Senator Obama did not know the words to the National Anthem or how to render the appropriate honor by covering his heart with his right hand. His campaign handlers likely instructed Senator Obama that if he were to win the state primaries and the nomination, he must not give the Republicans any chance to use propaganda against them. He needed to learn the words and protocols of the Pledge of Allegiance and the National Anthem before his next public outing.

Senator Obama, New Mexico Governor Bill Richardson, Senator Hillary Clinton, Ruth Harkin stand during the National Anthem[14].

The propaganda value of the picture and the video was significant for those on the right. It is likely that some former military members serving on the Obama Campaign recognized the political *faux pax* and took immediate corrective actions (counter-propaganda). Newspapers and networks across the country rarely showed the photograph without an official campaign explanation that Candidate Obama was politely listening to the singer of *The Star Spangled Banner*, or that the photograph was taken before he raised his hand to his to heart. However, the video clearly shows that throughout *The Star Spangled Banner* Candidate Obama simply stood with his hands in front of him[15].

Some would race to Snopes or others who pretend they are fact checkers for some words of refutation. But in those early days of the campaign, Senator Obama made it known in his books and interviews that he still knew the opening lines of the Arabic Call to Prayer from the Muslim schools he attended in Indonesia as a boy. It was also reported (if you knew where to look) that Senator Obama "...could recite them with a first-rate accent." Candidate Obama was also quoted as saying that, "...the *Call to Prayer* was the most beautiful sound he had ever heard[16]." Was this an odd characteristic for a self-described Christian or appropriate training for a future commander-in-chief? Counterterrorism specialists found the optics beyond belief and contemplated possible frightening scenarios. More on that later.

Following the many references to being able to speak Arabic and declaring that the *Call to Prayer* was "the most beautiful sound he had ever heard" some Americans found those comments to be sufficient evidence that the candidate (and later the president) was *taqiya*[17], the Arabic word meaning "one who denies their actual religious belief and practice."

This practice (*taqiya)* is emphasized in Shia Islam whereby adherents are permitted to conceal their religion when under threat of persecution or compulsion. For religious scholars this is a rare and unusual act. There are two main aspects of *taqiya*; avoiding the disclosure of association with the Imams when doing so may expose the community to danger or harm, and keeping the esoteric teachings of the Imams concealed from those who are not prepared to receive them. Some people suggested that Candidate Obama wrapped himself in the shroud of Christianity to hide his identity as a Muslim. We will look at those charges in a later chapter.

We will see that the media censored large parts of Obama's history: all the drugs he consumed as described in his autobiographies; being in *The Choom Gang*[18]; all the radicals he associated with, masking the importance of those relationships and dismissing Bill Ayers (the one standing on the American Flag, above) as "...just a guy in the neighborhood[19]." One could make a pretty good case that he was not the man the media reported him to be; they were caught in several cases of *lying by omission*. The media's version of *taqiya*: avoiding the disclosure of association with the media when doing so may expose the community to danger or harm.

Unlike the American media, the Democrat Party, and Hollywood, this book will not attempt to hide or distort the many discussions of the Founding Fathers regarding the requirements for president during the drafting of the U.S. Constitution. These debates and documents are recorded for history. Should the president's allegiance be to America and only America? Should the president be a "natural born citizen" (a child born of two U.S. citizens)? Or should the requirement for president be someone with no allegiance or a split allegiance to America, a "native-born citizen" (a child born within the boundaries of the United States)?

If such a case were to ever reach the U.S. Supreme Court, nine justices would be tasked to do what we have done here—review the related literature and historical documents and disregard the media's input and biased interpretation. They would determine what is Constitutional and what is not.

And above all, they would do it without propaganda.

CHAPTER 3
AMERICA'S MEDIA AND THEIR UNHOLY RELATIONSHIP WITH THE DEMOCRAT PARTY

The media play games when it comes to research and reporting. They pick and choose; they report what is in their best interests, what is directed by their leaders. They have a disconcerting way of ignoring adverse material when it comes to their people or candidates. This is media censorship without any of the warning labels. Above all, media is big business.

Recently and coincidentally, a *Non Sequitur©* cartoon by Wiley Miller captured the problem of living with a corrupt media. A guy at a bar with another man railed in frustration, "The older I get, the more disillusioned I get... It's just one big lie after another. The lies are easily refuted with facts, but we still hold on to them, not wanting to admit we were fooled by people we trusted."

Americans across the fruited plain have an expectation that the media's investigative research is comprehensive, total and accurate. That there is no need for them to lie. They tell the truth. Their research and reporting—if there is research and reporting done at all—is more like what contracting professionals call, "the lowest cost, technically acceptable" solution.

Average Americans have it in their power today to be able to research virtually any topic with a smartphone. If we can find something through research, even with limited resources, the media can too. If we need to know something, we will look until we find what we're looking for. Because we know that information is out there somewhere; we just have to find the right word or phrase to plug into a search engine in order to find the reference.

We can't wander into a newsroom or onto a set of network news, but we can watch the 1940 movie *His Girl Friday* to discover the lengths the media will go to get a story (research) and put it in front of the chief editor for publication. The comedy *His Girl Friday* has it all, a criminal wrongly accused of murder and condemned to die by hanging, competing reporters conducting research on a man they never met and relying on word-of-mouth of other reports—or reporters—as "evidence." Reporters are constantly on the phone filing their stories or tidbits of information with their editors. The reporters had assumed the accused man was guilty and deserved to die, so they wrote their articles supporting their conclusions without evidence.

When one of the reporters discovered information that exonerated the accused, she tried to stop the execution. She threatened to expose the mayor's corruption; he had been hiding the man's pardon. She even threatened to expose the police chief's incompetence of losing his gun during an interview.

The Rosalind Russell and Cary Grant comedy was famously funny, all while epitomizing and lambasting the dark side of the news media. The Rosalind Russell character was leaving the business because it was so corrupt. The Cary Grant—chief editor character—used criminals to neutralize good, honest people who got in his way by *creating the illusion* that *they* were engaged in some criminal behavior. Any innocents who were in the way of the master manipulator were arrested and thrown in jail. It was a way to *make news*, which is different than *reporting* the news. The Rosalind Russell character knew exactly what the corrupt Cary Grant character had done to her—framed her *husband-to-be* as a criminal—but she couldn't stop what she was doing. Conducting good honest journalism even amid a sea of dishonest journalists was addictive, like a narcotic. Before she knew the accused man was innocent, she finagled an interview with him in jail. It was an exclusive, and exclusives sell newspapers. She did whatever was necessary to find the truth. The corrupt journalists in the Press Room wouldn't be caught dead trying to find the truth. They were older men, cynical, tired, effectively retired from the business but still drawing a check.

His Girl Friday is a comedic look at the excesses of a corrupt media. Students of *dark psychology* are astounded to see the classic Machiavellian manipulator in the Cary Grant character—a loveable rogue doing whatever it took to get his way. The Rosalind Russell character tried to escape the corruption all around her, the craziness, but Cary Grant is such a powerful influence that she is sucked right back into it.

Consider the number of movies made about the media. There were dozens of movies about small but honest mom and pop newspapers in small towns that eventually got steamrolled by corrupt entities. Later, incorruptible journalists were turned into super heroes (like Clark Kent at the Daily Planet by day, Superman in any emergency) reporting on government corruption or criminals. One could say this is the way the media should be.

So why isn't it? Power is one reason. But the main reason is because the media is an unregulated business, and as an industry without oversight, it has become corrupt. First Amendment privileges with no industry or government oversight seems to allow a bad media to flourish and turn into a corrupt one. Good people who find themselves in a corrupt organization find ways to get out, leaving a vacuum to be filled with more corruption. When the corrupt learn the dark side of manipulation and mind control techniques, watch out, for they could soon be engaged in propaganda and selling Americans the idea that the Republicans are engaging in nonsense, such as claiming the Democrats are trying to run an ineligible candidate for president.

Why are the media corrupt? It would take a graduate course on ethics to separate the good media from the criminal. We suggest we have been the victims of persuasion, manipulation, and those mind control tools needed to generate what is called in *dark psychology*, an "Illusion of Truth." In certain circumstances, Machiavellian manipulators in media, like the chief editor-Cary Grant character in *His Girl Friday*, rise to prominence to become the fount of manufactured truths. Salacious stories sell; sob stories do not.

CNN dominated cable news for years, and other networks began using "CNN" as a reference in storylines. Meaning, the other networks didn't have to do the research CNN had done (or supposedly had done). All an anchor of a competitor's news show had to do was repeat what CNN had already reported—all because it supposedly had been vetted and approved. CNN became the headwaters of a story that others cited as their reference. You see this today on cable news networks and the newspapers.

We have seen these recent headlines:

CNN Director Admits Network Ran “Propaganda” to get Trump “Voted Out”[1]

Behind the Curtain: How the New York Times Manufactures Lies for Democrats to Attack Their Opponents[2]

There are many more examples.

When politics are in play—the media cannot and will not tell the truth, although they will try to create an “illusion of truth” for varying reasons. They will provide good coverage for the Democrat Party in exchange for access. Then, when they are through the gates and inside the wire, military talk for being in the building, inside the compound, the media become lapdogs.

Walter Duranty is the benchmark for a horrible journalist who traded positive coverage in exchange for access to a corrupt government. Duranty was an American journalist who served as *The New York Times* Moscow bureau chief at a time when access to the Soviet Union was nearly impossible. He was granted access and received a Pulitzer Prize for his glowing reports about the Soviet Union, all while ignoring the widespread famine in Ukraine.

The difference between creating an “illusion of truth” and “reporting what you see” is the media’s sole and awesome power to establish, define, and control “the narrative.” They write, shape, and form a story to comport with their chief editor’s or producer’s directions. If they don’t, the story does not get printed or broadcast. That story is “spiked” or is sent to “Edit” to make it fit the narrative of the paper or news service.

Another recent report of the media’s perfidy was:

Washington Post corrects report that Giuliani was warned he was target of Russian influence campaign-CNNPolitics[3]

When the goal was to get former New York City Mayor Rudy Giuliani, the media breathlessly reported his house had been raided by the FBI. Only it didn’t happen and retractions were the order of the day. With an honest media, that story would have never been printed; the publisher would have killed it before it ever saw the light of day, the reporter booted from the premises for shoddy reporting. Proof of the event, however, would have ruled the day...but that is not what happened. They tried to create a story that was damaging out of something that did not happen. Reporters played politics and got caught.

The media's treachery has been used since 2007 to benefit Democrats; it is only recently that some of the media's "journalistic excesses," a euphemism for BIG LIEs have come to light in conservative media.

"Illusory truth effect" by definition in *dark psychology*, is the tendency to believe false information is correct after repeated exposure. This effect is highly propagandistic. The illusory truth effect (also known as the illusion of truth effect, validity effect, truth effect, or the reiteration effect) was reportedly first identified in a 1977 study at Villanova University and Temple University.

That this phenomenon was *first identified* may be *illusory truth effect* at work. Studying the tendency of humans to *believe false information is correct* after repeated exposure was the purview of the master of mind control, Joseph Goebbels, the Nazi Reichsminister of Propaganda. This is not a joke. This simple understanding of the human mind is the essence for controlling it.

You tell a lie big enough and keep repeating it,
people will eventually believe it.
–Joseph Goebbels

This is the reason he is referenced throughout this book. The Goebbels' quote could be considered an example of an illusion of truth. His statements aren't some obscure 80-year old's observations subject to recent interpretations. They are statements from the master of propaganda. And these quotes are perfectly applicable to today's media and Democrat Party as they were in the 1940s.

The Ministry of Propaganda was in the business of mind control and finding ways of moving thousands of Jews to the gas chambers without resistance. Goebbels' statement was not *braggadocio* but a demonstrable fact. "*When* you tell a lie big enough and keep repeating it, people will eventually believe it."

The Nazis in charge of moving Jewish people to concentration camps proclaimed, that no harm would come to them, that they were being moved to a safer location. The Nazis put them under extreme pressure and they could not think straight. They controlled the Jewish people by manipulating what they believed. Today we know that was *the* BIG LIE, a monstrous murderous lie. Survivors of the death camps tell horrific stories of fellow Jewish people being beaten, standing for hours in the snow unable to flee or fight back. For a brief moment in time they had believed the lie and gotten on the train.

In the previous chapters we began to demonstrate that Barack Obama and his fellow Democrats knew that he wasn't eligible for the Office of the President. He didn't meet the constitutional requirements. A surprising number of Democrats in Congress not only knew he was ineligible but sought to quietly amend the U.S. Constitution to make him eligible. There were other eligible candidates the Democrat Party and the media could have supported, but they chose Senator Obama. The media could have killed Senator Obama's candidacy with an exposé on the simple fact that he was not born of two U.S. citizens—his father was from Kenya—but they didn't. We ask, "Why?" Was it to win an election with an amazing once-in-a-generation candidate or was there something more?

Once we assembled the pieces of the puzzle, we noticed that the media worked tirelessly to create an "Illusion of Truth," or an "Illusion of Legitimacy." The Democrat Party and their friends in media and Hollywood manipulated an unsuspecting America public during the 2008 presidential election. Yes, they used propaganda whenever they could try to create a clear case of, "Who are you going to believe? Us or the ramblings of some dead old men pictured on U.S. currency?"

That line, "Who are you going to believe? Us or the ramblings of some dead old men?" is a specific situation in a number of books on *dark psychology*. It is a method of persuasion, identified as "weapons of influence," and specifically defined as "Social Proof." When people find themselves in a complex social situation with limited or no information, they tend to consider the observable behaviors and choices made by a large number of people to be more valid than their own limited view.

It's a bit like what happens when exiting a subway car. If not familiar with the area, underground riders typically follow the flow of people as they leave the carriage. They assume the mass of people have no reason for trickery, that they are hardworking people trying to get to their place of business, and that they know where they are going. Society provides the proof.

The Jewish people in WWII Germany and Poland who followed the person or persons in front of them to the trains, to the concentration camps, and to the gas chambers demonstrated that "Social Proof" works. It was conceived by a master manipulator who knew how people's minds work, and it was executed to perfection.

"We all have problems recognizing the truth, but sometimes it's because we're dealing with manipulators. To make things worse, liars and manipulators are using the illusion of truth to convince us that what they say is fact. Their tactics seem to be working better than ever," said Sherrie Hurd, in her November 16, 2019 article, *The Illusion of Truth and How Liars and Manipulators are Using it to Trick You*[4].

Under the heading of *Yes, Kamala Harris is eligible to run for President*[5], the author of the piece cites a familiar refrain, and the media's response was almost verbatim what Barack Obama said when he ran for president.

"So, the key language is whether Harris is a 'natural born citizen.' And experts say she meets that definition." That is the extent of the media's research. "Experts say…." What the media really did was find a warm body with a law degree, pump him or her with a few bucks, beers, and bagels, and call that person an "instant expert." The *expert* said what the media wanted, a declarative statement with no research and no reference. If it isn't an expert, then it is a movie star or a sports figure who will do. All too many Americans accepted the statements without asking follow-up questions which would have likely exposed the lie. They followed the person in front of them, believing that the person who apparently knows the way or is famous in some way wouldn't lie to them. Such is the power of Social Proof.

The media cited constitutional scholars when they needed to preempt a line of questions. Who are these constitutional scholars? No one seems to know. They could be law school valedictorians or graduates of the bottom of their law school class. When the media comes-a-knockin' these lawyers should do some research instead of repeating what the media wants them to say. They should know they are being used, they should leave the beer on the bar, the bagels on the tray, and step away. Except the media's lawyers were addicted to the prestige of being a network subject matter expert. They were also hooked on the media's dollars.

Please know, we hold some lawyers in very high regard just as we do military pilots. There is a certain self-eliminating element for a bad pilot flying a jet. A bad pilot either quits because they cannot make any money, or they wind up killing themselves or others in a crash. A bad public defender or private practice attorney who cannot make enough money to survive often turns to politics or the media. Some of those featured in media outlets are paid millions of dollars every year by network news stations to be an on-call mouthpiece on the air. Ever wonder why there are dozens of lawyers as network hosts? This is how the media leverages *dark psychology's* "Social Proof." These lawyers are put on the air; people assume they know what they are doing and saying; people believe them. The master manipulators in the media are experts in knowing how to use "Social Proof" as a weapon; people will follow the media's expert out of the network offices like lemmings and if they say they should vote for a particular someone, the manipulators will get them into the voting booth.

These attorneys went to law school, but either they didn't learn the 1st, 2nd, 4th, or 5th Amendments and Article II of the U.S. Constitution or they ignored the law because the network, as the propaganda arm of the Democrat Party sets the narrative. The Democrat Party and media's narrative must be followed, otherwise all those super high salaries disappear as they are shown the door.

The media seem to become energized when dealing with criminals or ineligible presidential candidates, like Barack Obama and Kamala Harris. They hire a couple of lawyers to give credence to their claim (substantiation by another) and call it good enough. Instead of spiking a story that wouldn't get past the editor of a high school yearbook, the Cary Grant chief editor of the major newspaper trusts his guy, puts his imprimatur on the story, and ensures it runs on the front page. If it becomes necessary, they can always print a retraction to correct the record. But if they don't have to correct the record, the lie stands as written. This is "lying by commission" and can be very effective in slipping a verifiable falsehood past the censors or the spikers of stories.

The former CNN journalist and WMAL star, the great Chris Plante, reminds his listeners that, "...one of the most insidious powers the media possesses is the power to ignore." When a reporter submits a story on a political situation the network producer or chief editor may soften or harden the reporter's approach to the article, or as Chris Plante indicates, may spike it completely and ignore it.

At CNN, Chris Plante was a Pentagon Correspondent, Senior Producer for National Security Affairs, Military Affairs Producer, and an assignment editor. Plante traveled to foreign locations including Saudi Arabia, Bosnia, Vietnam, Indonesia, Africa and the remote corners of the former Soviet Union covering stories for CNN. He reveled in the perks of being a CNN Pentagon Correspondent: flying in high performance fighters, riding in submarines and carriers, and seeing the face of the enemy up close and personal.

For his reporting from the Pentagon during the terrorist attacks on September 11, 2001, Chris Plante received the Edward R. Murrow Award from the Radio Television Digital News Association. In 2003, he reported on Geraldo Rivera getting kicked out of Iraq[6] for "giving away the big picture stuff." Plante was ensconced at CNN and had been a lifelong Democrat until he famously acknowledged that he had seen the light and had left the Party. He realized that the media was corrupt, and he now uses his radio show to demonstrate how the media manipulates its readers and viewers, and distorts their reporting to maintain the network's or administration's narrative. Chris Plante and reporters who have defected from the left's networks know why a corrupt media does what it does best: they do not report on the truth, they are there solely to shape the narrative. A reporter's aim to report the truth with fairness is shunted by an agenda that maintains the political narrative.

If a presidential candidate (Obama or Harris) sputtered nonsense and gobbledygook when asked if they are a "natural born citizen," a good reporter wouldn't accept this bag of baloney and move on. A good reporter would sense the obvious evasion of the question. A good reporter would realize immediately the candidate was very reluctant to give a yes or no answer to a simple yes or no question. A good reporter would wonder why. A good reporter would ask follow up questions. But a compromised media would never let a good, honest reporter work on such a story, because ignoring the truth is the order of the day. The truth does not fit the narrative.

Gaining access to a candidate puts a reporter in a tenuous position. If the candidate disagrees with an article, the reporter is cut off and denied any further access. Candidate Obama was famous for kicking reporters off his jet, reporters who provided what the campaign perceived as a negative report. If an article advances the candidate's narrative the reporter becomes part of the media's lapdog kennel show. So, reporters learn quickly—if they want to fly on the jet and get access to the candidate, they had better learn how to spit tobacco to play ball. This is one way the political parties manipulate the media to get what they want—favorable coverage for their candidate and unfavorable coverage for the opposition candidate, even if it leaves a bad taste in their mouths.

These are not cases when a presidential candidate (Obama or Harris) would be better served by being truthful. If they declared that they are a "natural born citizen" when they obviously are not by any definition of the law, they would be guilty of fraud. This is especially relevant when documents are signed attesting that the candidates are eligible and qualified—not only to hold the office but also to receive government-provided campaign funds.

The Federal Election Commission (FEC) oversees laws that grant presidential candidates access to "campaign and campaign matching funds." Under the Federal Election Campaign Act (FECA) and the Presidential Primary Matching Payment Account Act, the FEC must certify to the Treasury that a candidate meets the enumerated statutory eligibility requirements to receive funds under the applicable act. This is where real laws are being broken. It is a crime to receive federal funds fraudulently; i.e., under false pretexts. Yet none of the FEC acts refer to the constitutional eligibility of candidates for federal office. Constitutional eligibility to hold office should be an implicit condition to certification for receiving funds under the Acts. How hard can this be?

Campaigns always need lots of cash. As presidential candidates, Obama and Harris could not tell the truth. They did not want to commit the obvious crime of fraud by attesting they were eligible and qualified for the office when they knew were not. So they chose to obfuscate or to have someone lie on their behalf, someone who would gladly take one for the team so the stream of government funds would keep rolling into campaign coffers. In a subsequent chapter, we will show the documents used by the candidate's campaigns did exactly that. We will also explore how the Democrat Speaker of the House of Representatives attested to the qualifications of Senators Obama and Biden to run for the office of president and vice president as required by the election laws in the 50 states. We have the documents. They show the conspiracy to elect an ineligible person was much greater than anyone ever imagined.

Americans assume that some government entity vets candidates to make sure they are eligible. Americans are not aware that each political party is responsible for vetting and certifying the constitutional eligibility of their own candidates for president. Some have likened this to asking the fox to guard the henhouse. If the Democrat Party says their candidate is eligible, then that person must be eligible. As we have seen, the Democrats have proved they were willing to take the FEC's money regardless of the qualifications of their candidates. This is a well-known gap in government policy that the unsavory are keen to exploit for their benefit. The government is not organized sufficiently to ensure only eligible candidates are considered for the office of the President of the United States.

There is no excuse for the FEC to allow this.

CHAPTER 4
WHY THE MEDIA WOULDN'T CONDUCT A STUDY

If the candidate's political views oppose a reporter's political views then nonsense and gobbledygook answers can be expected instead of yes or no answers. The Democrat Party handlers insist their candidates not be exposed to political malice in reporting. The media screen their people to ensure only *friendlies* ask the questions proffered and approved by the Democrat Party. They do not allow impromptu questions from *unfriendlies* which would be loaded with rational thought, the law, and constitutional disqualifiers.

In the 1950s, 1960s, and 1970s, no one in the media ever asked Democrat congressmen or senators what they or their constituents found so odious with the "natural born citizen" clause in Article II of the U.S. Constitution. If the U.S. Constitution was actually in error, wouldn't the natural question from an unfriendly media be, "What are you guys doing to fix it? Have you proffered any legislation to fix the presumed disqualifying issues?"

Another question would be, "If there is a real problem with the U.S. Constitution and the 'natural born citizen' requirement, instead of throwing no name lawyers in front of a camera or microphone to regurgitate Democrat talking points, case law on citizenship, why wouldn't the media conduct an actual study?" America would like to know if this is a real problem or a hypothetical one. Unquestionably, the media would say, "That's not our job." As we will see later, the media believes their job is to tell us what to think, which sounds suspiciously like a quote from *Mein Kampf* or Goebbels' Ministry of Propaganda. So, they create a mirage of facts, an "Illusion of Truth" complete with repetitive and overwhelming national coverage in television and newspapers.

Instead of allowing the media to dictate the narrative on potentially sensitive issues through sports figures and Hollywood sources, wouldn't it make sense for the network media to commission a board of professionals to include top federal immigration attorneys who were steeped in the knowledge of the U.S. Constitution? Then they could honestly report the findings. But the media would likely respond with, "Well, we can't have that! Then they'll want us to tell the truth all the time!"

The truth is simple, but lying and covering up those lies is complicated. They report, "And experts say he was born in Hawaii" or "She meets that definition." No specifics, no legal references. No law, no proof, no facts. This is the classic example of the media's "Illusion of Truth" effect at work. Any media-driven study would expose them as liars and Fifth Columnists.

Consider this, if there were something wrong with the definition of the "natural born citizen" clause, wouldn't one of the 204 law schools in the United States of America submit their discoveries to Congress citing all of the case law? Wouldn't they suggest a Congressional commission be promulgated to determine how and why the U.S. Constitution has been wrongly interpreted for over two centuries?

No law school, the scrutinizers and teachers of the U.S. Constitution, has found that the Constitutional document or the "natural born citizen" clause *is* wrong. This is because when something is and has been in the U.S. Constitution for over two centuries, it is *Constitutional.* However, about fifty authors of law reviews have *suggested* there may be *evidence* that the Constitutional *standard* "natural born citizen" might not be all that it could be. It might be unconstitutional! What they are arguing in essence is that a *standard* foot might not be twelve inches, it might be a liter. We'll discuss these in detail in a subsequent chapter.

The actual reason the media did not empanel experts to discuss and analyze the meaning of the "natural born citizen" clause was they already knew what the outcome would be for their candidate of choice. There was the little matter of no less than eight documented Democrat Party attempts to amend the constitution so Barack Obama could run as an eligible candidate. The study's conclusion would not support the narrative they were trying to manufacture. There would be no doubt or ambiguity in what the law provided.

Corrupt societies and organizations find ways of making their questionable or ineligible candidates acceptable. This is usually done through violence or cheating through the ballot box. America shuns violence, especially during an election cycle. We are a sophisticated first-world country. So, the media and the Democrat Party try to make the opposition believe *by force*. Recall:

Things must be ordered in a such a mode that when [men] no longer believe, one can make them believe by force.
–Machiavelli, *The Prince*

They don't use threats or dead bodies. They don't use reason or rationale. They use the weapons of influence found in the discipline of *dark psychology*. Propaganda is the most common method used to control how one person or a group of people thinks. Commissioning a study would be counter-productive.

When it fits the narrative of the left and the media, the Democrats do, on occasion, commission studies. These studies have *limited participation* in which *the outcome is predicted*. This outcome is always a conclusion which *proves their point*.

What does a *legitimate* study look like? The Center for Security Policy commissioned the "Team B II" study to look at the legal-political doctrine known within Islam as *shariah*. "Team B II" was made up of top security policy experts charged with looking at the preeminent totalitarian threat of our time, *shariah* law. This study challenged the assumptions and the policies of co-existence, accommodation, and submission that were rooted in those assumptions regarding violent extremism. Was it a problem or wasn't it? Documents surfaced that, when translated, suggested *shariah* was being purposely and quietly implemented in the U.S. The group was made up of experienced "security professionals," such as:

LtGen William "Jerry" Boykin, (former Deputy Undersecretary of Defense of Intelligence)
LtGen Harry E. Soyster, (former Defense Intelligence Agency Director)
Christine Brim, Chief Operating Officer, Office for Security Policy
Ambassador Henry Cooper, (former Director of the Strategic Defense Initiative)

Major Stephen C. Coughlin, Esq., (former consultant, Office of the Joint Chiefs of Staff)

Michael del Rosso, Claremont Institute and Center for Security Policy

Frank J. Gaffney, Jr., Center for Security Policy

John Guandolo, (former FBI special agent, counter-terrorism division)

Brian Kennedy, Claremont Institute

Clare M. Lopez, Center for Security Policy

Admiral James "Ace" Lyons, (former commander-in-chief, Pacific Fleet)

Andrew C. McCarthy, (former chief Assistant U.S. Attorney)

Patrick Poole, consultant on military and law enforcement anti-terrorism issues

Joseph E. Schmitz, (former Department of Defense Inspector general)

Tom Trento, Florida Security Council

J. Michael Waller, Center for Security Policy and lots of other stuff...

Diana West, expert and author on intelligence and counterterrorism

R. James Woolsey, (former Director of Central Intelligence)

David Yerushalmi, General Counsel, Center for Security Policy

A *Who's Who* of counterterrorism experts. This is what a real study commissioned by a competent authority looks like. The case of *shariah* was and had been a question for the intelligence community and counter-terrorism agencies. The expected response would not be a political response such as "the left sees *shariah* this way" or "the right sees *shariah* that way."

The Center for Security Policy sought straightforward answers from their panel of experts and those analyses were extensively discussed and debated. Their answers and conclusions were published as findings. There were no secrets, even though the topic was extremely sensitive. The Center for Security Policy's findings: SHARIAH: *The Threat to America*[1] and

"An Explanatory Memorandum," *From the Archives of the Muslim Brotherhood in America*[2], are available on Amazon.

Contrast that with the media buying the services of lawyers or the Democrats engaging with partisan hacks who report only what the Democrats allow. The Republicans engage with experts and professionals across the political spectrum. Think we're ideologues? Look at the last 100 studies conducted by each political party and then decide. We'll look at what the Democrat Party calls a study in a following chapter.

We have broached an important element of today's mainstream media. What our corrupt media does is eerily similar to what foreign intelligence agents (like the KGB or FSB) do to other intelligence agents. Foreign intelligence agents target American men and women for information, they want to acquire our national secrets by any means necessary. If our intelligence agents can be targeted and compromised, then a foreign agent will be able to get them to do exactly what they want. Our seemingly open and fair media does the same thing when they report compromised news as facts.

The media, who some say vote 98% Democrat, cannot engage in subjects where the proof is in the documents; a case in point is the *Naturalization Act of 1790*. In the case of Barack Obama, they were forced to use psychological mind control tools (propaganda, repetition of lies, lies by omission, etc.) to have any chance of dragging their ineligible candidate across the finish line.

This is why the journalism is considered one of the most dishonest professions on the planet and why the media is so reviled.

CHAPTER 5
WHAT THE LAW REVIEWS ACTUALLY REVEAL

The Supreme Court of the United States has not investigated or analyzed a finding or legal document on the topic of "natural born citizen" because there has never been a case brought before the court. The U.S. Supreme Court has seen many *citizenship* cases. But not cases involving the Constitutional *requirements for the President of the United States.*

So, we have to look elsewhere to find some legal or constitutional brilliance. For the record, we have already demonstrated that Snopes and the media are not founts of truth, but do whatever is necessary to maintain the left's narrative. They have no credibility. We need credibility. Which begets the question: is there a place where we can get good honest, trustworthy, and actual legal information and analysis? In other words, is there someplace that is *apolitical*?

Could an investigation and analysis of the "natural born citizen" clause begin with reviewing the products of law schools, the Constitutional law classes, and their law reviews and journals? Some of the nation's 204 law schools publish the research and analysis of students, professors, and faculty in their law reviews and journals.

A law review or journal is a law school publication containing both case summaries written by student members and scholarly articles written by law professors, judges, and attorneys. These articles focus on current developments in the law, case decisions, and legislation. Law reviews are edited by students, and students contribute notes to featured articles.

There are about fifty articles from different law schools on the topic of "natural born citizen," most of which were written in the last century. The nexus of media and the law review articles is obvious as they misreport on the topic of "natural born citizen." To truly get a sense of their perfidy in politics we must separate the articles into two categories:

Before Obama (<2008) and After Obama (>2008). There are one or two exceptions to the slant of reporting and political leanings.

Of the fifty, about forty articles challenged the Framer's intent of what is meant by "natural born citizen," and they all referenced one paper extensively: *Who Can Be President of the United States: the Unresolved Enigma*[1]. It was written by Charles Gordon and published in 1968 in the Maryland Law Review. Gordon's article was written when the father of Massachusetts Governor Mitt Romney, Governor George Romney, ran for President. Gordon let his readers know that George Romney was born to American citizens in a Mormon colony in Colonia Dublán in the state of Chihuahua, Mexico.

Gordon's article revived the legal concept of *jus soli*[2] (Latin: *right of the soil)*, commonly referred to as *birthright citizenship*. It is the right of a person born in the territory of a state to nationality[3] or citizenship. Gordon and other legal minds in similar law review articles rejected Governor George Romney's claim of Constitutional presidential eligibility as a "natural born citizen" based on *jus sanguinis*[4] (Latin: *right of blood*). In this principle of nationality law citizenship[5] or ethnicity is not determined by *place of birth* but by having one or both parents who are subjects or citizens of the state. This is their evidence. What does the law state?

What is most fascinating is that Gordon and other authors of articles show their political plumage by completely dismissing the law, the Constitutional *standard* of "natural born citizen" as the *children born to U.S. citizens* as found in the *Naturalization Act of 1790*. "Natural born citizen" is a *standard*; it can only mean one thing—a *child born to U.S. citizens*. There are other *standards*: a foot is twelve inches, not 11 or 13, a mile is 5,280 feet. A *standard* is not negotiable. In this case, "natural born citizen" is in the Constitution. Any deviation from "natural born citizen" is unconstitutional. It is for this reason that the left does not like "natural born citizen." They prefer another definition, one they can manipulate. They argue, through case law on *citizenship*, that a Republican candidate for president born abroad of U.S. citizens is not a U.S. citizen based on *jus sanguinis*. They argue citizenship is determined by *place of birth* under the legal concept of *jus soli*.

There is a simple reason that these law school professors and faculty dismissed the definition contained in the *Naturalization Act of 1790* in their articles (Before Obama). It seems that these articles were written to make a two-fold political argument. They cite various case laws involving ***citizenship*** in order to disqualify *Republican* presidential candidates (who are mentioned extensively in the law review articles) on the basis that it was incorrect to assume that they were a "natural born citizen" simply because they had been born abroad of American citizens. They also argue the U.S. Constitution should have read "native-born citizen" (*jus soli*). Thus, ignoring the Constitution and the *Naturalization Act of 1790*, and citing their chosen evidence, they conclude the presidential candidates born abroad of U.S. citizens should not be qualified as "*natural born citizens.*"

It's fascinating that these attorneys didn't have problems with the "natural born citizen" clause in between elections, before there were Democrat candidates that needed help in disqualifying Republican candidates, especially those who were born abroad of U.S. citizens. The problem arose only after these persons announced their candidacies for president. One wonders why that is. We have provided some links to the representative "Before Obama" Gordon-cited articles, here[6] and here[7]. They are numerous, and it's obvious they are intended to be political hit jobs and not scholarly work.

Where else have we seen this kind of sudden activity? Maybe when Congressmen Vic Snyder and John Conyers, Jr. got wind that a candidate needed some help to run for president –they just needed the U.S. Constitution amended. These Congressmen leaped into the fray to try and amend the Constitution to make their ineligible candidate eligible. Here, Gordon, *et al*, are doing the work for the Democrat Party, doing their part to put the imprimatur of legal scholar on a law review article in order to disqualify Republican candidates who were born abroad to U.S. citizens. Almost every article on "natural born citizen" cited in the law reviews can be found in their entirety from a Google search. Some obscure references required a Lexis Nexus search; our local library was able to get a hard copy of those at virtually no cost.

There are about ten law review articles, also Before Obama, that focused on a different topic entirely. They challenged the Framers' logic by claiming that the "natural born citizen" clause was *discriminatory*. They cited presumed evidence that the "natural born citizen" clause embodied

"...striking unfairness and dangerous ambiguity." If the "natural born citizen" clause was indeed *discriminatory* and *dangerous* and *ambiguous* wouldn't we have seen BREAKING NEWS as Democratic members of Congress racing breathlessly to the lectern with proposed legislation?

In *What Is the Constitution's Worst Provision?*[8] Robert C. Post argued that the Clause is highly objectionable because it unmistakably and clearly prohibits *naturalized citizens from becoming President* (emphasis added). Really.

And in *Unnatural Born Citizens and Acting Presidents*[9], James C. Ho argued that "No matter who wins the White House this November [2000], I and millions of other Americans like me once again will have suffered a certain measure of exclusion from the selection process. We have the right to vote, to be sure. But we cannot serve as President."

Let's review, why did no law school professors across the country make the case in their law school law reviews that the Constitution should be amended? Why didn't they propose that Congress should drop the "natural born citizen" requirement for president? Why didn't they argue that any person who has been a citizen of the United States for at least 20 years should be eligible to hold the office of President? Implicit and acknowledged in every one of these law review articles, even in lies of omission, is the unique constitutional presidential requirement that a "natural born citizen" is a person born of American *citizens*. Plural. Period.

Eighty percent of the authors of these law reviews argued that: there was evidence the Constitution was faulty, presidential requirements contained in Article II should have read "native-born citizen," and *Republicans* born abroad to American citizens should be *excluded* as presidential candidates[10]. Twenty percent of the authors argued that: *naturalized* citizens who were born (in the U.S. or abroad) to *foreign* parents should be *included* as presidential candidates, the U.S. Constitution's two century-old presidential requirements were a crime, and Article II, Section 1 was discriminatory. Not only was their evidence not convincing, it was unconstitutional. As far as we could ascertain, not one of these law review articles was ever made into a proposal to Congress in order to correct a faulty Constitution. The media would have covered the potentially earth shattering news with BREAKING NEWS morning, noon, and night.

Another article of note took a different tack on the "natural born citizen" clause. In her 1988 article (twenty years Before Obama) in the Yale Law Journal, *The Natural-Born Citizen Clause and Presidential Eligibility: An Approach for Resolving Two Hundred Years of Uncertainty*[11], Jill Pryor's abstract stated, "It is well settled that 'native-born' citizens, those born in the United States, qualify as natural born. It is also clear that persons born abroad of alien parents, who later become citizens by naturalization, do not. But whether a person born abroad of American parents, or of one American and one alien parent, qualifies as natural born has never been resolved."

Here we have someone trying to analyze a topic without doing the homework and looking at the related literature. Miss Pryor does not opine that Republican presidential candidates born abroad of U.S. parents should be considered "native-born citizens" or that the "natural born citizen" clause is somehow discrimatory. Like virtually all other opinions in law reviews, Miss Pryor opted to ignore the *standard* definition of "natural born citizen" found in the *Naturalization Act of 1790*. But she added a line in her abstract that had not been seen before in the other "natural born citizen" based law review articles. Curiously, it was not even discussed in her article. We repeat and truncate for clarity: "But whether a person born ... *of one American and one alien parent*, (emphasis added) qualifies as natural born has never been resolved."

Of course, we ask, "Since when?"

Upon reading this we were actually taken aback by the claim. In all of the law review articles on the question of "natural born citizen," only Miss Pryor (now an Obama-appointed judge) *mentioned*, "...whether a person born ... *of one American and one alien parent*, (emphasis added) qualifies as natural born has never been resolved."

In 2008, for the very first time in our nation's history, one of the political party's nominee for president had *one American and one alien parent*. Whether he "qualified as a 'natural born citizen' was never resolved." There didn't seem to be any doubt of the meaning of the clause from 2003 through 2008 when multiple Congressmen and Senators knew Barack Obama wasn't a "natural born citizen" because his father was a passport-carrying foreign national from Kenya. They had tried to amend the Constitution so he could run as a legitimate candidate.

During the 2008 election, the media and the law reviews tried to disqualify John McCain. The ridiculous law review article, *Why Senator John McCain Cannot be President: Eleven Months and a Hundred Yards Short of Citizenship*[12] led the way for another round of politically-motivated disinformation hit-jobs on a Republican candidate born abroad of U.S. citizens.

Miss Pryor's claim whether a person born abroad of American parents "qualified as a 'natural born citizen'" had also been "never resolved" was pure malarkey. We believe she relied too heavily on the findings of Charles Gordon's article which led her astray. She and Gordon *chose* not to include the definition contained in the *Naturalization Act of 1790*. In the end, she didn't make her case and came out of the process with less credibility.

She would have needed a crystal ball to see what happened during the 2008 election. Senate Resolution S.Res.511[13] "resolved" Senator John McCain's so-called questionable status (under Chin's and Pryor's articles) as a "natural born citizen." He was a person born abroad of American parents (the definition contained within the *Naturalization Act of 1790*) and Senate Resolution S.Res.511 officially resolved that he was a "natural born citizen." We will discuss this issue fully in a subsequent chapter.

However, and most noteworthy, during the 2008 election there were *no* members of the Senate willing to offer a Senate Resolution to resolve Senator Obama's on-going questionable eligibility as the Democrat Party's nominee for president. We will go into greater detail on President Obama's eligibility in subsequent chapters.

The outlier (in our estimation) to all of the law review articles is Christina Lohman's 2011 (After Obama) article in the Gonzaga Law Review, *Presidential Eligibility: The Meaning of the Natural-Born Citizen Clause*[14]. She examined the Constitutional clause and addressed the point of her research, "...whether the clause was intended by the constitutional Framers to include *foreign-born* (emphasis added) children of American citizen parents." She found and concluded:

Included are children born within the allegiance or jurisdiction of the United States. Children born to citizen parents who are in a foreign land as a result of United States government employment undoubtedly fall within the allegiance of the United States, and, therefore, are eligible for the Office of the Presidency. The Framers, however, had an even broader understanding of "natural-born." This understanding was reflected in a statute passed by the First Congress, of which twenty constitutional Framers were a part, that defined "natural-born" as including all foreign-born children of American citizen parents. Through this statute, the First Congress interpreted, at least in part, the constitutional meaning of "natural-born." As a result, all foreign-born children of United States citizens parents are eligible for the Office of the Presidency.

Christina Lohman's article is a meritorious and brilliant piece of legal research. She avoided the pitfalls, traps, and swindles of media and politics, both pre-Obama and post-Obama. She didn't ignore the definition contained within the *Naturalization Act of 1790* and she didn't try to manufacture a political case using citizenship case law on an issue of presidential requirements.

The whole topic leaves an oily residue. It makes one want to shout at the fifty or so law review authors. They chose poorly, wrote flawed articles with specious evidence (case law on *citizenship* is not the same), and censored the historical documents that didn't support their narrative. In other words, they conducted a fraudulent analysis based on outcome—they started with their conclusion and then looked at the related literature which supported that conclusion. That's not analysis or research. It is a waste of time.

Miss Pryor believed the propaganda as did many others who used Charles Gordon's article as a reference, not realizing *Who Can Be President of the United States: the Unresolved Enigma* had been crafted to be a political weapon against a Republican foe. It began with the conclusion that Romney wasn't a "natural born citizen" and then worked backward to try to prove it. She probably assumed Gordon's article was apolitical, thorough and accurate. But Gordon took a page from Goebbels' handbook on propaganda and created the BIG LIE—the Republican candidate who had been born abroad of U.S. citizens was ineligible, he was not a "natural born citizen," and thus could not run for president—that was the conclusion before there was any research.

Treachery comes in many forms. Politics compromised them to create a lie and then try to prove that lie. They had to ignore the Constitutional *standard* and make up one of their own.

CHAPTER 6
WHAT THE FOUNDERS ACTUALLY SAID; WHAT THE MEDIA CONVENIENTLY IGNORED

Now we are able to put everything we have discussed so far into its proper context.

The historical record of our Founding is a treasure trove of information. Alexander Hamilton had several heated discussions on this particular topic: should the requirement be "natural born" or "native born?" He convinced the Foundering Fathers and the writers of the Constitution and the Naturalization Acts *en masse* that any American president should have allegiance only to America. Being born in the country did not guarantee allegiance to the new Nation. Future American presidents should be born to people with allegiance to the United States.

ALLEGIANCE

When the Father is a: / And the Mother is a:	US Citizen	Foreign National
US Citizen	Allegiance is wholly to the USA	**Allegiance is split between the USA and a Foreign Country**
Foreign National	**Allegiance is split between the USA and a Foreign Country**	Allegiance is wholly to a Foreign Country

Recall that the *Declaration of Independence* was dated July 4, 1776. The Revolutionary War was fought between 1775 and 1783. Great Britain formally recognized the independence of the United States in the Treaty of Paris, on September 3, 1783 and two weeks later the U.S. Constitution was approved and signed. During all that time (1775-1783), there was much combat, intrigue, and political maneuvering between the newly declared independent United States and Great Britain. But early American history isn't taught in its entirety in schools anymore, so it isn't surprising that Americans today have little understanding of what happened then. They are not to be blamed for being confused by the "natural born citizen" clause.

Reviewing the old correspondence and the *Federalist Papers* brings awareness that these men were drafting some of the most perspicacious documents in all of the world for newly freed men, *United State citizens.* Only the *Magna Carta* in 1215 compares in its attempt to promise protections of church rights and illegal imprisonment, access to swift justice, and limitations on feudal payments to the Crown. There was resistance. The *Magna Carta* was annulled by Pope Innocent III, leading to the First Barons' War. Carl von Clausewitz said, "Politics is combat by other means." He wasn't the only person to notice that politics and war are intrinsically linked.

Unlike the weak protections promised in the *Magna Carta*, the *Bill of Rights* and the new Constitution were written in the strong "protective" language of the 1780s. Such as, "...the right of the people to keep and bear arms, *shall not be infringed.*" Very directive and unequivocal. Alexander Hamilton said words to the effect that to protect the United States one must have a leader who is dedicated to the new country and his fellow American. Presidents and politicians ensure allegiance to America when the chief magistrate is a proud, loyal, and dedicated citizen who works for the best interests of Americans and America.

America did not need another king. George Washington refused to be king. He believed a president should work for the security of America. Free men should elect their officials, not have those officials thrust upon them by force of tyranny. John Jay suggested and George Washington agreed that the leader of the military, the commander in chief, should be no less an American than a "natural born citizen."

How could the Founders ensure George Washington-like dedication and allegiance from those presidents who came after him? The brilliance of the Founders was on display again. It was as obvious as John Hancock's signature on the *Declaration of Independence*, being a "natural born citizen" must be one of the requirements for the Office of the President of the United States. No other term would do.

To be honored with such a high office, future presidents must be taught allegiance to the United States from their early days of childhood by mothers and fathers who were United States citizens. To ensure there was no ambiguity in its meaning or stature, this was codified in the very first set of laws that defined citizenship, the *Naturalization Act of 1790*. When a child is produced from either a mother or a father who isn't a United States citizen *allegiance* to America *cannot be guaranteed*. An American child is born with an allegiance to the country of his parents regardless of where they happen to be.

When we read the words of Alexander Hamilton, John Jay, or George Washington we are in awe of their specific use of the language of 1780. These men discussed the expected retaliation of King George III and his continuing threats to the new country. The Founding Fathers did everything in their power to draft, define, and document every possible means to prevent *foreign* agents from infiltrating and damaging the new government.

The men who signed the *Declaration of Independence* knew they would invite a declaration *and* an escalation of war from England. They knew they would be considered traitors to the Crown and would be essentially forfeiting all of their worldly possessions to King George III. In signing the document and serving in positions of authority they were putting bounties on their own heads. The King of England did not disappoint; he placed a bounty on the heads of those who signed the *Declaration of Independence*. Yet the signers concluded:

We, therefore, the Representatives of the United States of America, in General Congress, Assembled, appealing to the Supreme Judge of the world for the rectitude of our intentions, do, in the Name, and by Authority of the good People of these Colonies, solemnly publish and declare, That these United Colonies are, and of Right ought to be Free and Independent States; that they are Absolved from all Allegiance to the British Crown, and that all political connection between them and the State of Great Britain, is and ought to be totally dissolved; and that as Free and Independent States, they have full Power to levy War, conclude Peace, contract Alliances, establish Commerce, and to do all other Acts and Things which

Independent States may of right do. And for the support of this Declaration, with a firm reliance on the protection of divine Providence, we mutually pledge to each other our Lives, our Fortunes and our sacred Honor.

The signers of the *Declaration of Independence* outlined their complaints:

The history of the present King of Great Britain is a history of repeated injuries and usurpations, all having in direct object the establishment of an absolute Tyranny over these States. To prove this, let Facts be submitted to a candid world.

He has abdicated Government here, by declaring us out of his Protection and waging War against us.

He has plundered our seas, ravaged our Coasts, burnt our towns, and destroyed the lives of our people.

He has excited domestic insurrections amongst us, and has endeavored to bring on the inhabitants of our frontiers, the merciless Indian Savages, whose known rule of warfare, is an undistinguished destruction of all ages, sexes and conditions.

Thomas Jefferson, as the primary author of the *Declaration of Independence*, outlined the complaints of *foreigners* under the direction of the British King:

He is at this time transporting large Armies of foreign Mercenaries to complete the works of death, desolation and tyranny, already begun with circumstances of Cruelty & perfidy scarcely paralleled in the most barbarous ages, and totally unworthy the Head of a civilized nation.

He has constrained our fellow Citizens taken Captive on the high Seas to bear Arms against their Country, to become the executioners of their friends and Brethren, or to fall themselves by their Hands.

From Jefferson's masterpiece, we see the detailed impact of *foreigners* heading to the United States to help those already in the United States *involved in the works of death, desolation, and tyranny*.

Is it any wonder the left, the Democrat Party, and the media conspire to whitewash the efforts and impacts of *foreigners* not only dedicated to the destruction of the United States from the time of our Founding to the present day, but use propaganda to claim repeatedly *foreigner* is a despicable and discriminatory word? Is the word *foreigner* being so oft repeated in the Founding documents the reason the left, the Democrat

Party of today, and the media declare that the word *foreigner* is vulgar and exclusive? Is this why they employ various forms of propaganda so that people want to remove the word from official correspondence? For the propagandist word burners of 2008 and today, *foreigner* as a legal term has become a special target for elimination as has "natural born citizen."

Coincidentally, as this is being written the new presidential administration plans to do away with an "oath of allegiance" for new citizens. To wit: "Among the barriers to citizenship on the chopping block is the oath of allegiance[1]—which requires[2] citizens to 'renounce and abjure all allegiance and fidelity' with any other country and promise to 'support and defend the Constitution and laws of the United States of America against all enemies.'" Specifically, the new presidential action suggests they will: Eliminate barriers in and otherwise improve the existing naturalization process, including by conducting a comprehensive review of that process with particular emphasis on the N-400 application, fingerprinting, background and security checks, interviews, civics and English language tests, and the oath of allegiance[3].

Alexander Hamilton and the other Founders were extremely wary—so soon after the Revolutionary War—of any foreign influence seeping into the new government. The Founders, Hamilton, Jay and Washington, *et alia*, attempted to keep the spies, the criminals, the imposters, the fortune-hunters, the mercenaries, the pirates, and the formerly British out of the new government, but most of all they wanted to keep *foreigners* out of the presidency.

Why would the group of signers of the *Declaration of Independence* or the great minds who wrote the *Federalist Papers* be wary of *foreigners* gaining access to the new government? *Foreigners* seeking the highest office in the land were prevented from doing so for multiple reasons, mainly, because the perceived purpose of *foreigners* was not benign; the purpose of *foreigners* was to undermine and infiltrate the U.S. government for purposes of conquest or personal benefit. Not a good choice for president.

The Founding Fathers were learned men, masters of vocabulary and vernacular. Twenty of the Framing Fathers were members of the First Congress, and eight of them participated in creating and drafting the "natural born citizen" clause. Thomas Jefferson detailed the treachery of *foreigners* heading to the newly formed United States and those already in the colonies in the *Declaration of Independence.*

Candidate Obama's father was a *foreigner* under American law. An alien. A nonimmigrant. A person with a passport from Kenya. In looking for explanations how the 2008 election occurred and reviewing the related literature on the subject, Alexander Hamilton's words from the 1780s deserve more consideration:

Nothing was more to be desired than that every practicable obstacle should be opposed to cabal, intrigue, and corruption.

After reading the complaints directed to the King of England in the *Declaration of Independence*, the thoughts and ratiocination of the *Federalist Papers*, and the content and implication of the letters of the Founding Fathers it should be obvious to all that the goal of the Founders was to compose a set of impenetrable eligibility requirements for future presidents. There would only be one-way in. They intended that "every practicable obstacle" should dissuade or prevent a *cabal* (a secret political clique or faction), discourage *intrigue* (making secret plans to do something illicit or detrimental to someone or something), specifically by *foreigners*, and disqualify those men who made their living on *corruption* (dishonest or fraudulent conduct by those in power).

The Founders knew intuitively who would try to attain and abuse the power of government for their own purposes. By promulgating only a "natural born citizen" shall be eligible to the office of the president, they believed they would stop *foreigners* and nefarious men in their tracks. And they wrote the U.S. Constitution to state: "No person except a natural born citizen ... shall be eligible to the Office of President."

From the *Federalist Papers*: No. 68: *These most deadly adversaries of republican government might naturally have been expected to make their approaches from more than one quarter....* The Founders tried to ensure there were no backdoor approaches to office; no mercenaries, no spies, no *foreigners*, and *no sons of foreigners*. Had the U.S. Constitution been written differently, a child who was a "native born citizen" and who was the child of a *foreigner* had a chance at becoming the president. The widespread and colloquial use of "natural born citizen" became the Constitutional *standard*, not to be negotiated or reinterpreted. It was the primary obstacle and the ultimate barrier for *foreigners to cabal, intrigue, and corruption* in the new national government.

In the words of Christina Lohman, a top law school graduate, no one objected to foreign-born children of citizen parents being deemed "natural born citizens." There are no such discussions or records in *The Records of the Federal Convention of 1787*.

For two centuries, the Fourth Estate never once asked, "Why." Now, as a functioning Fifth Column, they ask, "How do we help you place and promote an ineligible candidate for the office of president?" No one will ever suspect us (the media) to *...make* [an] *approach from more than one quarter....with the son of a foreigner.*

For the record, the *Naturalization Act of 1790* was replaced by the *Naturalization Act of 1795*. The line "*the children of citizens of the United States*, that may be born beyond the sea or out of the limits of the United States, shall be considered as *natural born citizens*" was removed in its entirety from the new and improved Act. Law school students, instructors, and law review authors who lean left politically have jumped all over this particular line declaring that this is the evidence the definition of a "natural born citizen" in the *Naturalization Act of 1790* was "repealed" in their minds with the *Naturalization Act of 1795*. Apparently, with the replacement *Naturalization Act of 1795*, the U.S. Constitution was suddenly rendered faulty, vague, and—oh by the way—the term "natural born citizen" is not defined anywhere in the Constitution.

Let us look at the evidence and not take the word of the media.

Once again we repeat the insight of Chris Plante that "...one of the most insidious powers the media possesses is the power to ignore." Law school students, instructors, and law review authors conveniently ignored Congress' multifaceted power to define something only once. They also conveniently ignored Congress' power to remove without comment *surplus* wording in subsequent or replacement legislation. In fact, Congress removes *surplus* wording all the time, especially when a term or terms no longer serve the purpose of legislation. Once defined, must the government continue to define a standard? Do *definitions* or *standards* change *without comment*? No. Can definitions or *standards* be *repealed*? No. *Standards* remain constant and are simply redundant in subsequent legislation. Congress provides a new definition when required.

Constitutional scholar and attorney, Christina Lohman, writing for the Gonzaga Law Review, tackled the issue of *surplusage* in: *Presidential Eligibility: The Meaning of the Natural-Born Citizen Clause*[4], "With regard to foreign-born children of American citizens, the new act was substantially equivalent to the old, except the term 'natural-born' was omitted. While reasons for this omission are unknown, one could certainly posit that the legislature recognized a possible constitutional conflict and sought to correct it.... Yet, because it is unknown why 'natural-born' was omitted, it is premature to conclude that Congress did not consider such children natural born."

"When examining the broad picture of citizenship, the issue of insuring compatibility with the Presidential Qualifications Clause would not likely have jumped out as demanding attention. It is possible that since the 1795 Congress was farther removed from the framing of the Constitution than the First Congress, it simply did not recognize the significance of leaving 'natural-born' in the statute when it seemed to be *surplusage*." (Emphasis added.)

Not that the definition of "natural born citizen" was wrong and needed to be jettisoned like a bomb over Berlin in 1944, but that it was cluttering up the new and improved *Naturalization Act of 1795*. With every new Naturalization Act, must the government restate for Democrats with mental disorders the *standard* definition of "natural born citizen?" It was reasonable to remove historical or known definitions as "*surplusage*." Always remember, the Founders and members of the first Congress could have said in the Introduction to the *Naturalization Act of 1795*, "On the issue of presidential requirements, we believe the Constitution to be faulty; it should read 'native-born citizen' and the new Act of 1795 corrects the definition of the term *and the requirements for president in Article II of the U.S. Constitution!*" But they did not.

In all of *The Records of the Federal Convention of 1787*, you will not find any mention of any such conversation. It wouldn't make sense for them to have such a conversation. Law school professors and students writing for law reviews were more than a bit disingenuous! *Ignore only the definition of "natural born citizen" in the Naturalization Act of 1790*! The Democrats and the media were caught lying by omission.

In multiple efforts to disqualify Republican candidates born abroad to U.S. citizens, law professors writing for law reviews tried to make the case that the "natural born citizen" ***clause had been repealed*** and no longer applied. But notice the facts, there have been no "corrective" legislation, no amendments to the Constitution. The forty or fifty law professors and students who tried to make their case in their law review articles that the "natural born citizen" requirement in Article II of the U.S. Constitution was vague or wrong or discriminatory, *didn't succeed.* Neither did the congressmen who tried to amend the Constitution under false pretexts for Obama's presidential aspirations. QED.

The term "natural born citizen" has not been replaced by the term "native-born citizen." There has been no new and updated definition. No new Amendments to remove the "natural born citizen" clause. So we ask the forty+ brilliant scholars of jurisprudence who cited the *Naturalization Act of 1795* in their articles and ignored the *Naturalization Act of 1790*, "Just how did your argument turn out? Did the Congress change the meaning of 'natural born citizen' for you?"

No.

"Were the targets of your articles, the Republican candidates for president who were born abroad of U.S. citizens disqualified by the arguments you made in your law review articles?"

No.

"Has there been an amendment to Article II of the U.S. Constitution?"

No.

"Has the Archivist of the United States, the head of the National Archives, taken a bottle of 'Wite-Out®' liquid paper correction fluid, brushed over 'natural born citizen' in Article II of the U.S. Constitution, and penciled in 'native-born citizen' on the parchment?"

No.

There have been no such "corrections." "Natural born citizen" is the Constitutional *standard*. President Obama's father was a foreigner, thus making President Obama an ineligible candidate for president.

When asked such questions, the media, Democrats, President Obama, Senator Harris, and other confused attorneys respond as they usually do when they have to face facts. When a microphone is thrust into their face, they repeat their practiced words of obfuscation, "Look, I'm very clear-eyed about the fact that they are going to engage, as you said, in what they have done throughout this administration, which is just, let's just be very candid and straightforward, they're going to engage in lies, they're going to engage in deception, they're going to engage in an attempt to distract from the real issues that are impacting the American people[5]." The rest of the quote from Senator Harris is, "I expect they will engage in dirty tactics and this is going to be a knockdown drag out. And we're ready. And we're ready. There is so much at stake in this election and I'm prepared to fight, because this is a fight that is for something, not against something. This is a fight for where we need to be. And as you've heard me say many times, I'm very, very clear that we need to focus on what can be unburdened by what has been."

BLAME is one of the principles of propaganda. Debase, defame, dehumanize, defend. The ineligible blames others while claiming they are the victim, not the source of the conspiracy. Through the spectacles of *counter-propaganda*, citing the obvious truth that cannot be spoken, that cannot be spoken by an ineligible candidate, the quote is a long way from, "No, I'm not a natural born citizen" but the gobbledygook is loud and clear, "I want to be the next president; however, I cannot answer your question truthfully and remain a viable candidate."

The facts surrounding Kamala Harris are that she was born in America to a Jamaican father and an Indian mother. One parent may have been naturalized while the other parent was never naturalized.

The left and leftist lawyers try to make the legal case based on manufactured evidence that the Constitution and over two centuries of presidential elections are wrong, that these no-name new-wave law school flunkies' interpretation of the presidential requirements are correct. Add this to the list of "Illusion of Truth" effects. The media, Hollywood, and the Democrat Party do not have the Constitution or the facts on their side. They had NOTHING, so they had no choice but to revert to propaganda, disinformation, and outright lies to try to convince a trusting and unsuspecting public.

During President Trump's impeachment trial by the Senate, Harvard Professor Emeritus Alan Dershowitz told a group of future prosecutors: "If you have the law on your side, pound the law. If you have the facts on your side, pound the facts. If you have neither the law nor the facts on your side, pound the table."

All the law review articles wished to pound the table on this issue as a "hail Mary pass" to disqualify Republican presidential candidates who were born abroad. Christina Lohman's article comes to the rescue again with reason and aplomb.

"In addition, the Presidential Qualifications Clause requires the President to be a United States resident for fourteen years. It can be argued that this residency requirement contemplates foreign-born natural-born citizens and is designed to insure proper loyalties among these as well as other natural-born citizens. While the Presidential Qualifications Clause only requires natural-born status of those individuals not American citizens at the time of the adoption of the Constitution, the fourteen-year residency requirement applies to both natural-born citizens and those who were citizens at the Constitution's framing. Therefore, it is likely that Congress omitted 'natural-born' because they viewed the words as *surplusage*." (Emphasis added.)

We've thrown the term *citizen* around with "natural born citizens" and "native-born citizens" and "naturalized citizens." It would be good to look at who is and isn't a citizen, and what makes a citizen. Then we can look at presidential requirements as stated in the U.S. Constitution, and we can look at how the 2008 candidates, especially the media's chosen candidate, were treated by the media.

CHAPTER 7
CITIZENSHIP AND ALLEGIANCE

To fully understand what happened during the 2008 Presidential Election, we will review the American laws on citizenship and "natural born citizen." The U.S. Supreme Court would have done this if they had been given a case *McCain vs. Obama*. The nine justices would have reviewed the U.S. Constitution, the law (American and Kenyan), and the related literature on the topic.

Nationality law is the laws of each country. Each country defines the rights and obligations of citizenship within the jurisdiction of their country, (this will be important later) AND NOT the jurisdiction of any other country. It details the manner in which citizenship is acquired, as well as how citizenship may be lost. Irrespective of country or constitution, a person who is not a citizen of a country, and in our case a person who is not subject to the jurisdiction of America, is generally regarded as a *foreigner* and may also be referred to as an alien when there are issues of immigration and naturalization. Foreign national and illegal alien are technical legal terms, *standards* codified in U.S. law. There is more.

A person who has no recognized nationality or citizenship is regarded as "stateless." The United States government defines "naturalization" as the process by which U.S. citizenship is granted to a *foreign* citizen or national after he or she fulfills certain requirements established by Congress in the Immigration and Nationality Act. One requirement for naturalization is to renounce all allegiances to one's previous country.

Earlier we stated the definition of *jus sanguinis* (Latin: *right of blood*) as a principle of nationality law by which citizenship or ethnicity is not determined by *place of birth* but by having one or both parents who are citizens of the state. Children at birth may automatically be citizens if their parents have state citizenship or national identities of ethnic, cultural, or other origins. Citizenship can also apply to children whose parents belong to a diaspora and were not themselves citizens of the state conferring citizenship.

We have been introduced to nationality law where *jus sanguinis* contrasts with *jus soli* (Latin: *right of the soil)*, commonly referred to as *birthright citizenship*, as the right of a person born in the territory of a state to nationality or citizenship. Throughout the world *jus soli* is used under very limited conditions such as when a child has been abandoned or has unknown parents[1]. Native-born citizenship is the predominant rule as an unconditional basis for citizenship in the Americas, but it is rare elsewhere. Since the Twenty-seventh Amendment of the Constitution of Ireland was enacted in 2004, no European country grants citizenship based on unconditional *jus soli.* Every country has its own constitution and within those documents the qualifications for citizenship are explicitly defined.

For example, the eligibility requirements to become a citizen of Mexico is[9]:

A. Mexicans by birth are:

I. Those born in the territory of the Republic, regardless of the nationality of their parents:

II. Those born in a foreign country of Mexican parents; of a Mexican father and a foreign mother; or of a Mexican mother and an unknown father;

Every year Democrats lobby for children who are born in the U.S. of Mexican nationals and insist they are automatically granted U.S. citizenship, although under the Mexican constitution these children are considered Mexican nationals. Democrats ignore the citizenship requirements of countless countries when it comes to making potential U.S. citizens. We will see how the Democrats and the media ignored the citizenship of Barack Obama's Kenyan father.

Unlike the majority of other countries, the United States accepts both *jus sanguinis* and *jus soli* people as citizens. One may be granted citizenship by being born in the United States, or by having a parent who is a citizen of the United States. These are *qualifications* for citizenship, not to be confused with the Constitutional *requirements* to be or serve as president.

Both the late John McCain and Barack Obama were born to at least one American parent who was a legal citizen of the United States at the time of their birth under *jus sanguinis.* John McCain and Barack Obama were/are U.S. citizens by virtue of the fact that their mothers were U.S. citizens and U.S. citizenship was automatically conferred to them as children under *jus sanguinis.*

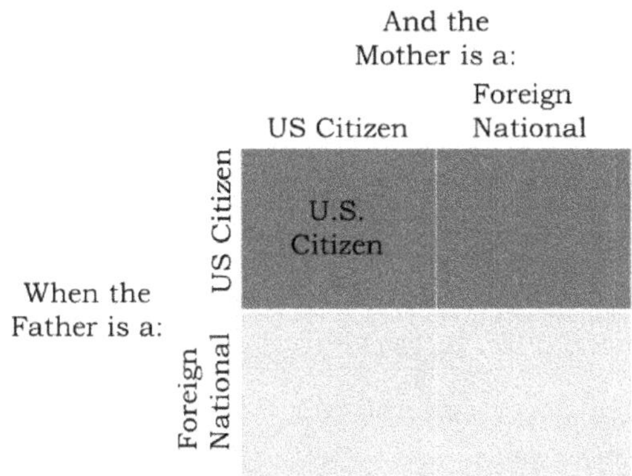

A child born to United States *citizens* is a U.S. citizen. For purposes of eligibility to become president, that child also falls into an exclusive category, conferred by an act of law (specifically, the *Naturalization Act of 1790*) as a "natural born citizen," a child born of U.S. citizens. Children born in America to American *citizens* are not required to be registered at birth. Parents are given a certificate of live birth to attest to the birth of their child. This certificate serves as the child's basic identity document.

A child born to a parent who is a *United States citizen* and a parent who is a foreign national, is not only a U.S. citizen as granted by *Immigration and Naturalization Acts* and under the concept of *jus sanguinis,* the principle of nationality law by which citizenship or ethnicity is determined by a parent. But in consonance with the citizenship laws of the foreign parent's national constitution that child is also a citizen or a national of the foreign national parent's country. These concepts are simple. They should make complete sense.

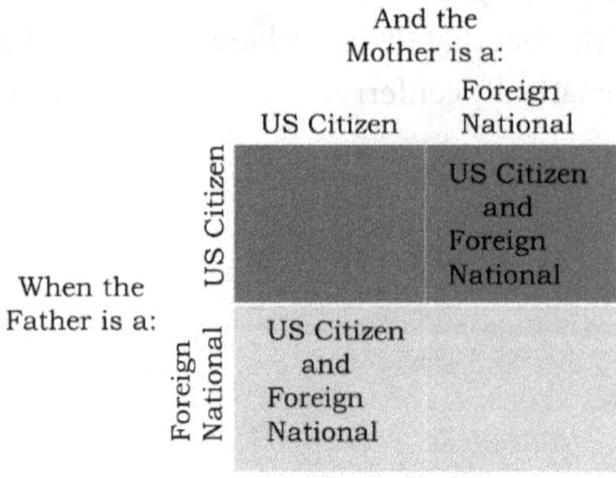

If a child is born to a United States citizen and a foreign national by birth, that child is recognized as a citizen of a foreign nation and is thus disqualified from being the President of the U.S. That child is not a "natural born citizen," a child born of U.S. *citizens* since one parent is a legal *foreign* national. Such children are subject to their parent's immigration and naturalization laws and subsequent citizenship laws. These children are persons with two legal citizenships; they are subject to the jurisdiction of two countries. They have legal responsibilities to comply with the laws of their parents' two countries.

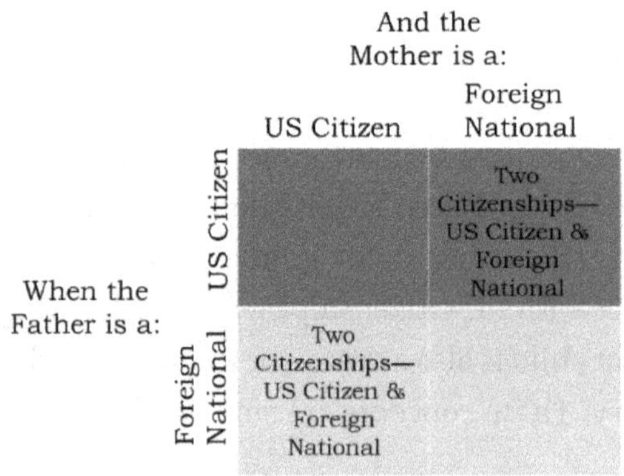

Under U.S. Immigration Law of the 1930s, John McCain's parents were required to register their newborn's birth in Panama with the U.S. Embassy. In the 1960s, under the Kenyan constitution, Barack Obama's father was required to register his newborn's birth at the Kenyan embassy in the United States within 90 days of his birth. Both of these children had been "born abroad" ("born abroad" meaning Panama for the McCains and the United States for the Kenyan Barack Obama, Senior). Because official passports to travel (to Panama for the McCains and the United States for the Barack Obama, Senior) would not be issued to newborn children, those newborn children's pictures would be placed on a rider on a separate page in a parent's passport, typically the mother's passport but not always. It could take a few months for passports to be submitted and officially changed. Normally the passport would be taken apart and new pages sewn into the passport to reflect that a baby would be travelling with its passported parent.

It has never been in dispute that John McCain and Barack Obama were/are American citizens. The issue has been meeting the special Constitutional requirements when seeking the Office of the President.

No person except a natural born citizen, or a citizen of the United States, at the time of the adoption of this Constitution, shall be eligible to the office of President...

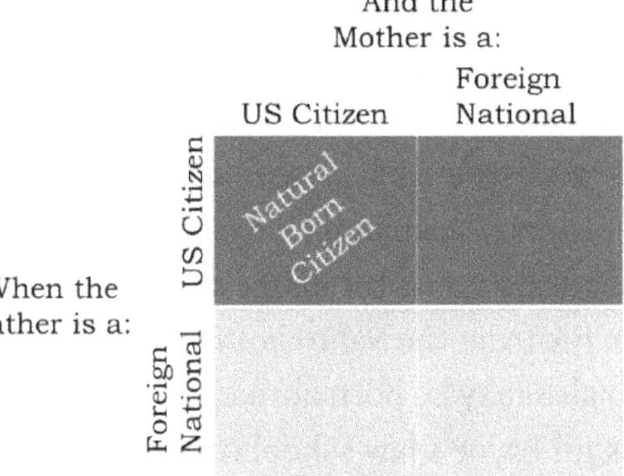

The term "natural born citizen" is a *standard*, an idea or thing used as a measure, norm, or model in comparative evaluations. *Standards* are exact, precise, and do not vary. Alexander Hamilton brilliantly established a Constitutional *standard*—a child born of two U.S. citizens is considered a natural born citizen—as the penultimate requirement for the office of the presidency; Congress codified it with the *Naturalization Act of 1790*. Once a *standard* is defined by law, any repeating of the standard is regurgitation. Congress makes a law and deigns that a mile is 5,280 feet long and doesn't have to mention how long a mile is every time that particular *standard* is mentioned in legislation. A *standard* not being mentioned or repeated in the *Naturalization Act of 1795* or any other piece of legislation means nothing. Repetition in law of a *standard* that has previously been defined is unwarranted and surplusage. A *standard* is not open to political interpretation. Laws have wiggle room and gray areas. *Standards* do not.

A Constitutional *standard* may not help a certain political candidate. If that candidate cannot meet the *standard*, one can try to change the *standard* through formal procedures or engage in some informal or illegal actions to make it appear your candidate meets the *standard*, such as falsifying official affidavits.

When Senator John McCain became the Republican Party's nominee for president, *the question if being born abroad of U.S. citizens* made one a "natural born citizen" and thus eligible to the Office of the President of the United States was resolved and affirmed with the April 10, 2008 Senate Resolution S.Res.511. The resolution wasn't necessary; the Senate reaffirmed the *standard*, the definition of "natural born citizen" in the Naturalization Act of 1790. S.Res.511 was *reassurance* of an obvious fact. A "natural born citizen" is a condition distinguished and defined by being born of two U.S. citizens, and nothing else.

Please note, the unanimous Senate Resolution (McCain abstained) thoroughly discredited and rejected those who claimed the U.S. Constitution was wrong or was discrimatory or should have read "native-born citizen." It reaffirmed the Constitutional *standard*, the definition of "natural born citizen" on file from the *Naturalization Act of 1790* as a person born of U.S. citizens who also may be born abroad of U.S. citizens.

Another look at Miss Jill Pryor's law school thesis suggests it was not politically motivated, as it was written well before Obama. We believe she suggested a theoretical dilemma. Could a person born of one American and *one alien parent* ever be considered a "natural born citizen?" Would legal action or legislation be necessary to resolve the hypothetical problem? If a candidate born of one American and one alien parent wished to have the question of eligibility resolved before running for president, the candidate has the right to challenge the constitutional requirement in court. We doubt such a lawsuit would go very far. This is also one of the functions of the Federal Election Commission. If you don't know if you are or are not a "natural born citizen," the FEC reviews the available facts and issues a decision. An ineligible candidate seeking FEC presidential campaign matching funds would commit a fraudulent act. A crime.

Despite Jill Pryor's understanding of citizenship laws of foreign nationals, natural law had resolved this issue many years ago and well before Senator Obama blasted onto the political scene. A person born of one American and one alien parent is and has always been recognized as a *dual national*[2].

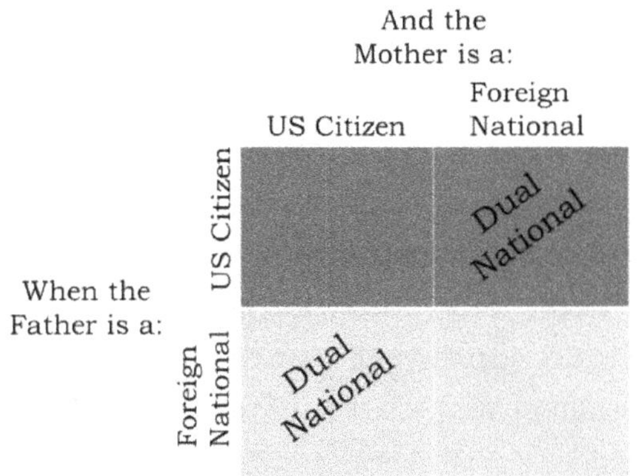

A *dual national* is defined as a person with two citizenships; a person who, like his or her American parent, is subject to U.S. jurisdiction as well as the jurisdiction of the other parent's country's laws. There are other ways to be a dual national, but for the purposes of this discussion in this chapter the written record reflects that the newborn child Barack Obama II was born of a foreign national (Obama, Senior, of Kenya and holding Kenya passport #84764) and an American citizen, Stanley Ann Dunham.

Whereby a *dual national* is a person born of a foreign national and an American citizen, even by his own admission in his autobiographies Barack Obama II was the son of a Kenyan national, making him a dual national, a citizen of two countries by birth, regardless of what the ladies on *The View* have rationalized when pleading their case for Obama's eligibility to be president. In their defense of Obama's lack of eligibility credentials, the ladies on *The View* seemed to be channeling Leni Riefenstahl, known for producing Nazi propaganda, and Joseph Goebbels that, "If you tell a lie long enough, it becomes the truth." This fact alone disqualified Barack Obama II for the office of the president.

And there should be no controversy. This is the truth. Paraphrasing Jack Nicholson, *Democrats can't handle the truth.*

Dual national is another term not defined in the U.S. Constitution but its definition is found elsewhere. Let's look at the official documents from the U.S. State Department.

The concept of dual nationality means that a person is a national of two countries at the same time. Each country has its own nationality laws based on its own policy[3].

There is no qualifying concern about *the location* of birth of a person born of a foreign national and an American citizen. Place of birth of a dual national child is immaterial—*jus sanguinis* applies. To reiterate, a dual national at birth is a citizen of two countries under the concept of *jus sanguinis*, not *jus soli.* And because a *dual national* is the citizen of two countries *simultaneously* it stands to reason, as in a Logic 101 course, dual national children are not born of two *U.S. citizens*, and are not "natural born citizens." Per the U.S. Constitution, they do not meet the *requirements* for the office of the president and are therefore ineligible to become president or serve as President of the United States.

In the eyes of the Constitution and the *Naturalization Acts*, the facts of the case could not be more clear: the 2008 Democrat Party nominee for president, Senator Barack Obama, was a man born of a foreign father so was not a "natural born citizen" as required by the U.S. Constitution. Upon his live birth in Hawaii, he was classified as a *dual national* by the immigration laws of two countries. His birth certificate listed his father as born in Kenya. Meaning Barack Obama, Senior was a *foreigner.* He received permission to enter the U.S. and was issued a Kenya passport. The U.S. State Department considered him to be a "nonimmigrant" and issued him a student visa—category F.

Barack Obama II was a citizen of his father's country until such time as he no longer claimed allegiance to the country of his father, unless other extenuating circumstances existed, such as his mother claimed him to be a *dual national* of another country, such as Indonesia. The Kenyan constitution reveals Barack Obama II was eligible to be the President of Kenya, but under the U.S. Constitution he wasn't born of two U.S. citizens, and therefore wasn't eligible to be President of the United States. Different countries have different qualifications and requirements for their presidents.

The media and the Democrat Party were familiar with U.S. laws but were likely ignorant of laws of foreigners who were subject to the jurisdiction of their own country. Barack Obama, Senior was designated a temporary visitor to the United States and was in America only to attend school, not to get married or have children. After five years in the U.S., he was unable to get his immigration status changed and was deported back to Kenya in July 1964.

During the 2008 election, when the media ascertained the sheer scope of the problem of the Democrat Party running an ineligible candidate, their focal point became how to make the ineligible candidate "acceptable" in the eyes of the Constitution. Eight attempts to amend the Constitution did not pan out. Telling the truth was an immediate disqualifier. But creating an "Illusion of Truth" or an "Illusion of Legitimacy" by the repetition of untruths and other persuasion and manipulation methods from the dark-side of psychology might help the candidate of their dreams reach the White House. The law and the facts were on the side of the Republicans. The media and the Democrat Party's only course of action was to "pound the table." Cue the media's thrumming and repeating their Goebbelsesque lie: Barack Obama II *is* a "natural born citizen." Remember, out of the mouth of the master:

If you tell a lie long enough, it becomes the truth.

–Joseph Goebbels

There is only one problem; even the Nazi's greatest propagandist determined that you could only maintain the fiction for so long before the lie collapsed on its own weight.

To assist and support the candidate of their dreams, Democrat media personalities, scholars, and politicians began ringing alarms and moving the goalposts. They attempted to redefine the U.S. Constitution's "natural born citizen" clause, claiming it was nothing more than "a relic of Eighteenth Century concerns that had little relevance to modern America." No law cited, no specifics, just platitudes and throw-away lines. As Obama's ranking improved in the primaries, there came a point where it was conceivable Obama could win the Democrat Party's nomination. That was the point the media determined Americans could not be told the truth. But Americans liked to see proof. Would propaganda be able to save their candidate from destruction? The media leapt into the fray to protect their candidate with an increasing crescendo of disinformation designed to distort or conceal the facts that Barack Obama's father was from Kenya, thus making the Barack Obama II a dual national.

Some Americans knew Obama wasn't a "natural born citizen." They went to court. The media and the Democratic National Committee attacked any who asked questions and those who brought lawsuits. They began constructing an "Illusion of Legitimacy" with perfect political obfuscation. The propaganda was breathtaking. They ignored the fact that Barack Obama, Senior was a liability and the disqualifying factor for his son's presidential candidacy.

The media conducted full-scale psychological operations, using the various principles of propaganda on the American public. Propaganda's BIG LIE and the "Illusion of Legitimacy" became media doctrine and established their narrative. Repetition of untruths, deflection of truths and facts, and disinformation became the new media normal. When that didn't work as well as they hoped, they shifted to a new BIG LIE and began using another *dark psychology* practice. They used various charges of racism to flip the dynamic, sow confusion, and upend the discussion.

Obama became their victim of racism. Charges of racism are very powerful. These unfounded accusations were solely designed to inflict mental anguish. For Barack Obama to have a chance to win, Americans needed to be reprogrammed, forced to think in a different way. The media moved from reporting the news to engaging in raw propaganda and leveraging other tools of *dark psychology*. The main source of their propaganda was direct charges of racism which were repeated over and over and in Hollywood. They would not address the issue, only decry some version that racists did not want to see a black man as the President of the United States.

Overnight, Republicans became the party of virulent racists. Network anchors engaged in racial histrionics: "Only a racist would question the bona fides of the first African American nominee for president." Hillary Clinton said frequently that Republicans were trying to delegitimize the first African-American president. They claimed that racism was the only reason the Republicans were questioning the *bona fides* of the Democrat Party's nominee.

The focus of the writings of the Founders: Hancock, Jefferson, Hamilton, Jay, Washington, and all of the others, was to keep *foreigners*, spies, criminals, imposters *and their sons* out of the new government. The Founders demanded the president have two U.S. parents and total allegiance to the United States of America. They were extremely concerned that foreign powers could "*gain an improper ascendant in our councils*" by "*raising a creature of their own to the chief magistracy of the Union.*"

Does "*raising a creature of their own to the chief magistracy of the Union*" suggest there could be an underlying tangential dynamic on the level and direction of *allegiance*? Does "raising a creature of their own" imply that a foreign parent with allegiance to a different nation could raise their child with an allegiance different than the one expected by the Founding Fathers? Was allegiance to another country or *split allegiance* the defining impeachable factor which would prevent a foreigner from achieving the office of the president? Could it have been something else, such as religious allegiance? Could it have been meant to encompass "both?"

Rarely mentioned by the media was the fact that Barack Obama, Senior was a Muslim. The concept and definition of *jus sanguinis* (Latin: *right of blood*) is the principle of nationality law by which citizenship or ethnicity *or religion* is not determined by *place of birth* but by having one or both parents who are citizens of the state or of the national religion of the state. Some references cite that, "Children are not born out of any sin, original, inherited or derived. They are born on the religion of their nature, i.e., Islam[4]." The Muslim Barack Obama, Senior transferred his religion to his son, Barack Obama II. The transfer of the father's religion is a global standard practiced in the Jewish religion, in the Hindu religion, in Islam and others.

We will see later where Barack Obama, Senior told the Foreign Student Advisor[5] of the U.S. university he was attending "...that in Kenya all that is necessary to be divorced is to tell the wife that she is divorced and that constitutes a legal divorce." This is a distinctly Muslim practice in Africa and the Middle East, not in Indonesia, for example. The point here is to offer evidence that Barack Obama, Senior, in body and soul, was a bona fide Muslim practicing Islam, when it suited him. When he announced he had married Stanley Ann Dunham, he was challenged that he already had a wife. He asserted he was divorced in the Muslim way as an Islamic divorce can take place by saying one time "I have divorced you" (*talluqtuki*) or "You are divorced" (*anti taliq*)[6].

A person who becomes a U.S. citizen through naturalization is not considered a natural born citizen[7]. Consequently, naturalized U.S. citizens are not eligible to become President of the United States or Vice President of the United States, as established by the Presidential Succession Act[8]. However, there is a case to be made that a child of naturalized U.S. citizens (those who have renounced their citizenship elsewhere) would be considered a "natural born citizen," for that child would be born to *American* citizens. Remember James C. Ho lamenting, "No matter who wins the White House this November [2000], I and millions of other Americans like me (naturalized citizens) once again will have suffered a certain measure of exclusion from the selection process. We have the right to vote, to be sure. But we cannot serve as President." But your children might.

Foreigners could renounce their allegiance to their former country as a pretext to infiltrate the U.S. government. *Foreigners* have used all sorts of designs to "gain an improper ascendant in our councils." The Founders believed if *foreigners* truly sought refuge in the United States, renounced their citizenship and allegiance of their home country, and became naturalized citizens of the United States, their children would be U.S. citizens and considered "natural born citizens." These children would be eligible to become the president.

Citizenship is heady business and should not be taken lightly. It is not the role of the political parties or the media or Hollywood to determine who is eligible for the office of the president. It is the role of government to determine who is a citizen and who isn't. Many countries define the eligibility requirements for president in their constitutions.

Let's stay with Mexico's constitution as an example. The eligibility requirements to be President in Mexico is[9]:

I. To be a Mexican citizen by birth, in the full enjoyment of his rights, and the son of Mexican parents by birth.

II. Mexican nationality is acquired by birth or by naturalization:

A. Mexicans by birth are:

I. Those born in the territory of the Republic, regardless of the nationality of their parents:

II. Those born in a foreign country of Mexican parents; of a Mexican father and a foreign mother; or of a Mexican mother and an unknown father;

III. Those born on Mexican vessels or airships, either war or merchant vessels.

Unlike Mexico and other countries, the U.S. Founders, primarily Alexander Hamilton, used de Vattel's 1758 legal treatise, *The Law of Nations,* to determine the Constitutional *standard* and describe the eligibility requirements to be president in three little words: "natural born citizen."

CHAPTER 8
THE STUFF WE'RE NOT SUPPOSED TO TALK ABOUT

There are several books that reference and describe "The Deep State" as an apolitical, subterranean, loosely defined structure that dictates national security decisions, policies, and priorities. Balderdash. There is nothing apolitical about the domestic enemy that is primarily made up of the Democrat National Committee (DNC) and their friends in the media, or their use of propaganda to achieve their goals. The Deep State also includes a few Republicans-in-name-only, RINOs, those politicians that outwardly identify as Republicans but inwardly are more like Democrats.

Contrast the Deep State with the *dark state* which is *extremely political*, and members of the *dark state* have the highest security clearances and accesses in government and they include Fifth Column media. The *dark state* knows secrets like how to wield propaganda like Thor's hammer.

Propaganda?

It is as if the *dark state's* knowledge of and use of propaganda is not to be discussed or even mentioned. Most Americans know propaganda is the nasty stuff the Nazis used against the Germans and the Jewish people. They even had a Ministry of Propaganda. But those days are over, right? We are at peace. Propaganda is not something Americans use, is it?

The *dark state* brandishes propaganda as well as the Nazi *Riechsminister*, Joseph Goebbels, did in the 1930s and 40s. The infrequent and measured use of propaganda is one key to the *dark state* Democrat Party and the media's success in getting their message to the people and keeping their people loyal to them.

Another key to the *dark state's* success is their top-level security clearances. They have access to the nation's most sensitive secrets and are able to dictate Democrat Party-led policies and priorities without regard for the actual interests or desires of the American people. It was *dark state* actors who took to the floor of Congress and quietly proposed amendments to the Constitution to eliminate a constitutional phrase that disqualified their chosen candidate for president.

The *dark* side of the media is right in the middle of the *dark state*, as part of the Democrat Party-media complex. Like-minded media icons—the CEOs of the major and cable networks and the legacy newspapers—assist the *dark state* at every turn. These are very powerful political people who work in the background.

Is this unfair? Read this headline from a major news website: BREAKING: CNN Executive ADMITS Propaganda to Defeat Trump![1]

If that assertion is true, it only confirms our assertions. This admission that the media used propaganda against a sitting president came straight from the mouth of a CNN executive. In the early 1940s and 1950s, such an admission would have seen the media executive prosecuted for treason. Was that admission simply hyperbole? How is it possible that the media could conduct such dastardly propagandistic operations? Let's look at an apolitical organization conducting very political operations.

The Department of Defense has Psychological Operations Groups that deploy on short notice wherever they are needed. They plan, develop, and conduct civil affairs and psychological operations in support of unified commanders, coalition forces, or other government agencies as directed by the National Command Authority. Some Americans may be surprised by the methods and techniques used by the Department of Defense and the intelligence community. One of the oldest military psychological operations (PSYOPS) ever recorded can be found in an August 11th, 1927 Chicago Daily Tribune article[2] which chronicled a propaganda method, a behavior modification technique, specifically *deterrence*, of burying "Mohammedans" with dead pigs.

The article stated that the practice discouraged fanatical "Mohammedans" who carried out suicide attacks against Christians while shouting *Allahu Akbar*; *God is great*. The Spaniards were the first to publicly bury corpses of suicidal Islamic cult members called *juramentados* (an old Spanish term used to describe Islamic suicide attackers) with the blood of slaughtered pigs. It was a tactic used to deter further suicide attacks, as it was a form of propaganda used to control the minds of suicide attackers by threats of violence against their beliefs. The *juramentados* were willing to give up their lives to kill an infidel, but they were not willing to engage in threats of violence against their beliefs. Killing an infidel meant they would go to Paradise; affronting them with the blood of swine, which was against the Quran, would deny their entry to Paradise.

When U.S. armed forces were deployed to the Philippines in 1927, the *juramentados* immediately began to carry out suicide attacks against U.S. forces. American officers were aware of the Spanish's use of behavior modification and propaganda tactics, and found the practice of using swine offal and blood an effective *deterrence* to the unprovoked suicide attacks.

Propaganda is based on controlling what people think. Propaganda is one of the *silent weapons* of *dark psychology*. When American soldiers killed these religiously-motivated suicide attackers, their commanders held very public funerals for them, which is more propaganda. Since the "Mohammedans" were to have no contact with swine and especially not its blood, the American soldiers threw the dead *juramentados* into a grave. Pig's blood was splashed over the dead from head to toe. Once the dead pig was thrown in the grave the burial was complete. The scene shocked any captured *juramentados*. Soon the word got out to not attack the Americans. However, that wasn't the end of the process.

General John "Black Jack" Pershing reported that his soldiers sprinkled captured *juramentados* prisoners with pig's blood and set them free to warn others. He was quoted, "Those drops of porcine gore proved more powerful than bullets." General Pershing controlled the minds of the *juramentados* with threats of being immersed in pig blood. This was raw battlefield behavior modification technique and it had the desired effect. Most importantly for American soldiers, the religiously-motivated suicide attacks stopped. This was a classic *psychological operation*.

Psychological operations have been conducted in the field of battle and post-war for a very long time. General Pershing's operation against the *juramentados* was almost a hundred years ago. What do psychological operations look like today?

Psychological operations (PSYOPS) are those methods and procedures used to convey selected information and indicators to audiences to influence their emotions, motives, and objective reasoning, and ultimately the behavior of individuals, groups, organizations, and governments. The Department of Defense (DOD) is not only in the business of warfare, they are also in the business of *psychological warfare*: developing, perfecting, and using mind control and behavior modification techniques in order to neutralize an adversary or to control an adversary's population in a manner of their choosing.

The internet has several websites describing military psychological operations that were used in Iraq, Somalia, Serbia, and Kosovo. One resource on the web is for the 9th Psychological Operations Battalion (Airborne)[3] at *www.psywarrior.com* which relates an outstanding history with photographs of PSYOPS products and the equipment used for conducting psychological operations on behalf of American and coalition forces. Psychological operations specialists engaged in information delivery to Somalia and Iraq, running newspapers and radio stations, and setting up radio broadcasting systems. These specially trained military personnel designed, printed, and distributed leaflets, posters, handbills, and generated pamphlets and booklets in the language of the country where U.S. forces were openly engaged in fighting the enemy of the people. These publications addressed various health concerns, such as malaria, sanitation, food preparation, and hand washing.

The majority of psychological operations used around the globe are informative by design ("white" psychology) and have achieved positive results. They inform the people in the middle of a military conflict what help is available and where it can be found, i.e., a booklet on how to conduct personal sanitation when the water treatment plant was destroyed in the war. The people were told where to find medical troops to take care of the ill and the infirm. These medical personnel delivered babies, fixed teeth, and set broken bones without the intimidation factor of weapons or armed guards at every corner. This created good will. These are examples of "white" propaganda.

Another example among thousands, as part of a Joint Psychological Operations Task Force, soldiers created "decreasing support" for Osama bin Laden in Afghanistan and encouraged hostile Taliban forces to leave Kabul or surrender. In Iraq, targeted PSYOPS decreased support for Saddam Hussein and encouraged hostile Baath Party forces to leave Baghdad or surrender. Controlling the narrative will cause the mind and body to follow. These are examples of "gray" propaganda.

Some media was necessarily negative, like printing posters or airing radio broadcasts that illustrated the crimes committed by Kosovo's Slobodan Milosevich or Iraq's Saddam Hussein and his sons. Much of this was *counter-propaganda* necessary to oppose the propaganda used by Milosevich or Saddam Hussein. Explicit photographs of past atrocities of Milosevich and Hussein were designed to shame the population and create distress. These were "black" propaganda programs, designed to alter thinking.

We saw these *counter-propaganda* efforts in black and white films when U.S. or coalition troops liberated the Holocaust survivors from places like Auschwitz, Buchenwald, Dachau, and Ravensbrück. The films forced the surrounding population of these towns to acknowledge the Nazis had lied to them. The films provided proof of what actually occurred. Tours of the death camps and the films were designed to disclose the evil their sons and fathers had committed in service to the Reich in the name of Adolf Hitler. It was painful to conceive of such evil. These *counter-propaganda* efforts shattered the minds of many German survivors. They did not want to know. This was purposeful and also *dark psychology* in action.

Look at the government's psychological operations websites and read what these specialists were doing and why. These post-war civil action activities were designed to shift the local government's inculcations that Americans in uniforms were there to cause harm. The indigenous people had been bombarded with negative propaganda; Americans extensively used *counter-propaganda* to create the perception that Americans were there to liberate and help. In other words, positive propaganda.

Is this really how *dark psychology* is used? How does it work in a free country like the U.S.? Consider someone who has become a target of the media and is accosted by a reporter. That person must brace for impact, because this is an *interrogation* technique designed to break a person's spirit. The person can step up to the reporter and submit to the media. Or the person can slap the microphone down and walk away. That is the effective *counter-propaganda* measure. Reject the media; say nothing. Leave them thinking they made a mistake and *These are not the droids you're looking for.*

The media recoiled in mock disgust from anyone who committed the imaginary crime of questioning the *bona fides* of Barack Obama. The media's actions were pure propaganda: *How dare you question the BIG LIE!* People who asked questions were destroyed financially, professionally, and mentally.

This is the secret of propaganda: Those who are to be persuaded by it should be completely immersed in the ideas of the propaganda, without ever noticing that they are being immersed in it.
–Joseph Goebbels

The media knew exactly what they were doing, just like any KGB-trained torturer hanging out at the Hanoi Hilton. Whoever questioned Barack Obama's eligibility would be reported on camera or in print as the vilest racist to have ever walked the planet. The implication is that fighting back creates humiliation and pain. Applying *counter-propaganda* measures by saying nothing or saying, "We'll see you in court," is not easy. Sufficient numbers of people were intimidated to never again inquire, however discretely or indirectly, into the background of the 43rd president. The use of *dark psychology* and propaganda by the *dark state* were seen in their full effect. People felt shame at being called a racist, however obliquely. The media recognized who could be controlled and who could not, those who shut up and disengaged and those who fought back. Those that fought back were threats to their narrative and must be destroyed by whatever means.

The media and the left are not above *re-labelling* descriptive items to achieve maximum leverage. For example, *enhanced interrogation techniques* become the reviled and hated *torture*, with the addendum *that it does not work*. This re-labelling implies *all enhanced interrogation techniques must not work*, especially when the subject matter expert testifying to his experiences was a famous prisoner of war. The Democrat Party lionized the service of Commander McCain and trotted him out to rebut the effectiveness of another very special mind control technique called waterboarding.

A captured terrorist is usually unwilling to talk to his captors and give up his secrets. Threats of violence will not change these people's minds. Like the suicidal Islamic cult members of a 100 years ago, the *juramentados*, these people would rather die than submit to their captors. These are learned behaviors.

It should not be a surprise to anyone that the Nazi Ministry of Propaganda investigated how to get a spy to talk without killing him or allowing him to kill himself. This is *dark research.* They found that the human body has certain natural reflexes that make the mind believe death is near. The will to survive is the strongest of these reflexes. The drowning reflex is one of these and is demonstrated in a training environment to members of the Special Operations Command to prepare them if they are ever captured and subjected to *enhanced interrogation techniques.* These methods and procedures are designed to make the captive think they are on the edge of death. The will to survive is great, and to prevent another round of simulated drowning the captured will eventually talk. The Nazi Ministry of Propaganda understood the mechanics and mind control methods behind what the media refers to as *enhanced interrogation techniques.*

We are familiar with one of the *enhanced interrogation techniques* known as waterboarding. Khalid Sheikh Mohammed, the self-proclaimed mastermind of the 9/11 attacks, was reportedly waterboarded 183 times. Al-Qaeda facilitator Zayn al-Abidin Muhammed Hussein, better known as Abu Zubaida, was reportedly waterboarded 83 times. Abd al-Rahim al-Nashiri who headed al-Qaeda's Persian Gulf operations, was said to have been waterboarded three times.

When WWII was nearing the end, the British and American intelligence community who had worked on dramatic operations such as stealing an Enigma machine from a Nazi U-boat, breaking the Nazi's Enigma machine code, and stopping Hitler's atomic weapons research, just to name a few, probably made a run on the Nazi's Ministry of Propaganda if they had been able to get there before the Soviets, and removed the files on all of their research. Reports of mind control experiments and other brain manipulation techniques carried out on death camp prisoners filled hundreds of boxes. Research that could have only been conceived and carried out in a totalitarian country could now in the hands of the Allies. If there was a theme to the Nazi's research it was, "We have ways of making you do whatever we desire." It would have taken years for the Allies to complete the study of the archives of the

Ministry of Propaganda, if U.S. forces were able to get to them. The research could be expected to contain elements of *dark psychology* and mass manipulation techniques that could not be replicated in a free society. There are very few resources on the subject that have been declassified, but in those that have, the intelligence community called these procedures and methods the *silent weapons in a quiet war.*

If it can be agreed that the media and the government are knowledgeable of the effects of *dark psychology* and how to properly apply propaganda protocols on the individual, then these same media and government organizations must be knowledgeable of the effects of *dark psychology* on the masses. The American talk show host and political pundit, Mika Brzezinski[4] was caught on camera saying of President Donald Trump, "...he could have undermined the messaging so much that he can actually control exactly what people think. *And that, that is our job.*" (Emphasis added.) This is exactly what we've been saying. The truth comes out only when the media slips up or are caught bragging on a hidden video recorder. The media lied and cheated and they used *dark psychology* to accomplish the goals their political lackey friends could not.

It is the absolute right of the State to supervise the formation of public opinion.

–Joseph Goebbels

What more evidence do you need? The media's stated mission is to control exactly what people think. Their mission required advanced PSYOPS techniques. They created and leveraged disinformation to inculcate the American people with well-crafted half-truths in order to first develop an "Illusion of Truth" and then created an "Illusion of Legitimacy" out of whole cloth while also forming a psychological alliance with the Democrat Party. The Fourth Estate was not the only Fifth Column, so was the Democrat Party.

We enter parliament in order to supply ourselves, in the arsenal of democracy, with its own weapons. If democracy is so stupid as to give us free tickets and salaries for this bear's work, that is its affair. We do not come as friends, nor even as neutrals. We come as enemies. As the wolf bursts into the flock, so we come.

-Joseph Goebbels

Is it fair to say that the media, as part of the media-Democrat Party complex, reports more favorably on Democrat Party issues than Republican Party issues? Is it fair to say that the media-Democrat Party complex is not above squelching unfavorable Democrat Party issues? Is it fair to say that the media will always report unfavorable Republican Party issues? Is it reasonable to expect that the media would actively engage in thwarting Republican Party issues when the Republicans have a distinct advantage over the Democrat Party? Yes, at every opportunity. The media, the Democrat Party, and even National Public Radio[5] would indeed do so.

Psychological operations are a vital part of the broad range of U.S. political, military, economic, and ideological activities used by the U.S. government to secure national objectives. Persuading rather than compelling physically, these entities rely on logic, fear, desire, or other mental factors to promote specific or desired emotions, attitudes, or behaviors.

The media are masters of propaganda, and they also engage in the classified works of mind control, persuasion, and manipulation by using their expertise in *dark psychology* to control the minds of the masses.

CHAPTER 9
REPUBLICAN PRESIDENTIAL NOMINEE SENATOR JOHN MCCAIN

An April 2000 report by the Congressional Research Service and constitutional scholars interpreted the phrase "natural born citizen" to include citizens born outside the United States to parents who are U.S. citizens under the "natural born" requirement of the U.S. Constitution. Democrat lawyers had debated the "natural born citizen" clause in law review articles as a way to disqualify Republican presidential candidates born abroad. In the 2000 presidential campaign, Senator John McCain's eligibility to seek the office of the president had been only a minor topic of conversation. The Wikipedia entry for John McCain[1] can be found here and the link is in the References section.

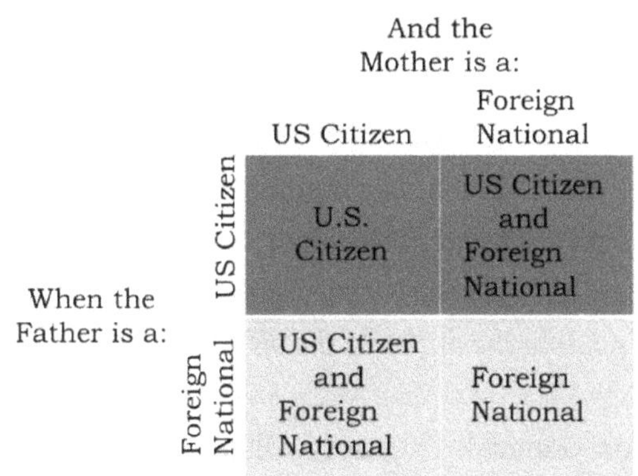

During the 2008 election cycle, the media and the Democrat Party tried everything they could to disqualify Senator John McCain as a presidential contender to Senator Barack Obama. They conducted opposition research, read books on *dark psychology*, and drafted journalists who had served with government psychological operations units and the classified mind control work of the intelligence community. Because politics is combat by other means, Democrats declared war and subjected

McCain's presidential campaign to a whisper campaign stating he wasn't eligible. It wasn't true of course, but that didn't stop the ethically-challenged Democratic Party from trying.

By virtue of being born of U.S. citizens, Senator John McCain was qualified and eligible to become president. But as we shall see, some Democrats in law schools insisted he wasn't a "natural born citizen" for various questionable reasons. They suggested there was evidence to the contrary. Panama was not part of the United States at the time John McCain was born. Under the concept of *jus soli*, the right of a person born in the territory of a state to nationality or citizenship, Gabriel Chin claimed John McCain was not a U.S. citizen but a Panamanian. In *Why Senator John McCain Cannot be President: Eleven Months and a Hundred Yards Short of Citizenship*[2] he ignored the obvious and cited the ridiculous. In 2007, Chin was the latest Democrat who failed to make his case in a law review article that was more drive by shooting than scholarly work. No one ever took up the challenge or took McCain to court.

John McCain's *allegiance* to the United States was always assumed, implied, and inferred because he was born of U.S. parents, was a career U.S. Naval officer, a former prisoner of war, and a U.S. Senator. In all previous government positions, in promotions in rank, and upon entering the U.S. Senate he had taken the Oath of Office:

I John Sidney McCain, do solemnly swear (or affirm) that I will support and defend the Constitution of the United States against all enemies, foreign and domestic; that I will bear true faith and allegiance to the same; that I take this obligation freely, without any mental reservation or purpose of evasion; and that I will well and faithfully discharge the duties of the office on which I am about to enter: So help me God.

Former U.S. Solicitor General Theodore Olson, a Republican, and Harvard Law professor Laurence H. Tribe, a liberal Democrat, undertook the task of researching the issue[3] of McCain's eligibility. Entitled "PRESIDENTS AND CITIZENSHIP Opinion letter by Laurence H. Tribe and Theodore B. Olson;" the full letter is appended in the Exhibits section at the end of this book. In their March 19, 2008 memorandum the two seasoned attorneys concluded that, "Based on the original meaning of the Constitution, the Framers' intentions, and subsequent legal and historical precedent, Senator McCain's birth, to parents who were U.S. citizens serving on a U.S. military base in the Panama Canal Zone in 1936, makes him a 'natural born citizen' within the meaning of the Constitution."

That should have been the end of the Democrat's shenanigans, but some people just will not believe the Constitution is not only straightforward but it is ***The Constitution***, the ultimate authority and official word for the United States.

However, Olsen and Tribe also threw in superfluous language and a Democrat Party talking point regarding *Senator Obama's eligibility*; specifically, paragraph 2, lines one and two of the Tribe and Olson Opinion Letter: "The Constitution does not define the meaning of natural born citizen."

This is not only a superfluous statement without meaning (i.e., the Constitution is not a dictionary) it is Democrat Party *propaganda*. This statement, repeatedly uttered or written, was designed to make the reader question the veracity of the Constitution, and as a consequence, shield the author of any article, opinion, or proposal to amend the Constitution. They made an *insinuation*. They didn't lie, but they didn't tell the truth either. This *insinuation* was repeated again and again, often enough, that constitutes propaganda.

A lie told once remains a lie but a lie told a thousand times becomes the truth.

–Joseph Goebbels

Of course, they knew that the Constitution does not define the meaning of natural born citizen. For that definition, they could have started with Emerich de Vattel's 1758 legal treatise, *The Law of Nations*. They could have consulted the *Naturalization Act of 1790*. They could have read the correspondence of the Founders in *The Records of the Federal Convention of 1787*, the Federalist Papers, and the newspapers from the time of the drafting of the Constitution.

But they ignored the historical record so they could *insinuate* that the drafters of the Constitution were unmitigated imbeciles who unbelievably forgot to define "natural born citizen." This is the essence of disinformation. Purposeful and propagandistic.

There is some additional mystifying language, specifically paragraph 5, lines 11 through 15 of the Tribe and Olson Opinion Letter: "Barack

Obama was born in Hawaii on August 4, 1961—not long after its admission to the Union on August 21, 1959. We find it inconceivable that Senator Obama would have been ineligible for the Presidency had he been born two years earlier."

Here are two supposed learned men, acknowledging Senator McCain was a "natural born citizen," the son of two U.S. citizens. At the same time they are validating *jus sanguinis*, we find them putting their fingers on the scale for *jus soli!* They ignore the actual definition of a "natural born citizen" and openly advocated for a new one: *ignore any contribution of the foreign parent.* They advocated that being born in Hawaii was sufficient to qualify Senator Barack Obama as a "natural born citizen." Thus he was eligible to run for President of the United States. Where is it written anyplace in U.S. law currently or in the past 240 years that the son of a foreign national is a "natural born citizen?" This is legal malpractice.

These two very experienced attorneys are talking out of both sides of their mouths. The first line of the second paragraph of their memorandum reads, "The Constitution does not define the meaning of natural born citizen," yet the final paragraph of the opinion *concludes*, "Based on the original meaning of the Constitution, the Framer's intentions, and subsequent legal and historical precedent, Senator McCain's birth to parents who were U.S. citizens...makes him a 'natural born citizen' within the meaning of the Constitution."

There is no need for propaganda to be rich in intellectual content.

-Joseph Goebbels

On April 10, 2008, Democrat Senator Claire McCaskill, [MO] sponsored U.S. Senate Resolution S.R.511 declaring Sen. John McCain—a former U.S. Navy Commander, a former Prisoner of War, and the son of an admiral—a "natural born citizen" and thus, he was fully eligible to run for and hold the office of president. S.R.511 stated that John Sidney McCain, III, is a "natural born citizen" under Article II, Section 1, of the Constitution of the United States.

S.R.511 passed 99-0—the unanimous consent of the Senate with only John McCain abstaining. Was this some kind of political trick? Maybe there was something in the wording of the Resolution. "*Whereas John Sidney*

McCain, III, was born to American citizens," a condition not met by Barack Hussein Obama II. Co-sponsors of the Resolution were DNC Presidential candidate Sen Hillary Rodham Clinton, [NY]; DNC Presidential candidate Sen Barack Obama, [IL]; Sen Patrick J. Leahy, [VT]; Sen Jim Webb, [VA]; Sen Tom Coburn, [OK].

But what do we really have here? Just as one must read the full Declaration of Independence to get to the complaints the Founders had with the King, one must also read the language at the bottom of the McCain resolution: *Whereas the Constitution of the United States requires that, to be eligible for the Office of the President, a person must be a 'natural born Citizen' of the United States;—Whereas the term 'natural born Citizen,' as that term appears in Article II, Section 1, is not defined in the Constitution of the United States.*

So that was their strategy. This was a BIG LIE.

Every line in the Constitution is a directive; there are no definitions. Take a look. Just declaratory statements. Pick any part. We are familiar with Article II, Section 1; let's look at that part again. To wit:

No Person except a natural born Citizen, or a Citizen of the United States, at the time of the Adoption of this Constitution, shall be eligible to the Office of President; neither shall any Person be eligible to that Office who shall not have attained to the Age of thirty five Years, and been fourteen Years a Resident within the United States.

Article II, Section 1 doesn't state, *No Person except a natural born Citizen, a term that is not defined in this Constitution of the United States so Democrats can devise a plan of action to present a candidate sometime in the future who is not a natural born Citizen, or a Citizen of the United States, at the time of the Adoption of this Constitution, shall be eligible to the Office of President; neither shall any Person be eligible to that Office who shall not have attained to the Age of thirty five Years, and been fourteen Years a Resident within the United States.*

We have set the record straight with the law and facts, and it is worth repeating. The U.S. Constitution is not a dictionary. The *Naturalization Act of 1790 mandated* that "*the children of citizens of the United States*, that may be born beyond the sea or out of the limits of the United States, *shall be considered as natural born citizens.*" (Act of March 26, 1790. 1 Stat. pages 103, 104 [emphasis added]).

To use red herrings and insinuation to sow confusion and doubt is a despicable act; to continually repeat it is propaganda. These mind control methods used by the media and the Democrat Party were perfected within the halls of Goebbels' Ministry of Propaganda and come directly from the pages of *dark psychology*.

If it matters, in an April 10, 2008 statement, Sen. Patrick Leahy (D-VT) chairman of the Senate Judiciary Committee, said, "Based on the understanding of the *pertinent sources of constitutional meaning,* it is widely believed that *if someone is born to American citizens anywhere in the world* they are natural born citizens. *Because he was born to American citizens,* there is no doubt in my mind that Senator McCain is a natural born citizen."

Senate Resolution 511 placed the focus on Senator McCain's eligibility to be president without addressing the obvious ineligibility of Senator Obama. The Senate chose to do nothing for Senator Obama. They would not go on record with a resolution that would not pass. No one wanted to be seen as *criticizing*, however tangentially, an African American Senator who seemed to not have the sense to realize he wasn't eligible. It may be fair to say no senator wished to be the arbiter of the question of Obama's eligibility. Through propaganda, the Democrats and the media had made the topic radioactive. The Senate would not be the ones to disqualify an ineligible black man. Let him fail on his own volition.

The Republicans seemingly took for granted that Senator Obama's 2008 candidacy would go nowhere based on his lack of *bona fides*. They knew he was ineligible going back to 2003/4 with at least eight failed attempts to amend the Constitution; they knew he couldn't win. He was likely running for third or fourth place in order to secure a cabinet position if Hillary Clinton won the election, as expected. The Republicans did not take the ineligible senator's candidacy seriously, for everyone in Congress knew he was ineligible. No one asked the Congressional Research Service to investigate the question of Senator Obama's eligibility to hold the office of the president.

Sometimes we have to look at the problem from a different vantage point. At the time of his birth, *if* John McCain wasn't a natural born citizen of the United States then what was he? The good news is we do not have to manufacture evidence to fit our narrative. John McCain was the child of American citizens in a foreign land *that had no claim to him*. John

McCain's father was on official duty in Panama and *but for* those official foreign duties, the infant John McCain would likely have been born in the United States.

Under nationality law and hundreds of constitutions, children born to ambassadors and military members who are abroad (and others, such as teachers, travelers, and *journeyers*) are citizens (or subjects) of their parent's country. It seems these distractors had a difficult time distinguishing the difference between an immigrant and a *nonimmigrant.*

The United States formally defines *nonimmigrants* under U.S. Immigration Law. Nonimmigrants[4] are foreign nationals admitted temporarily to the United States within classes of admission that are defined in the Immigration and Nationality Act (INA). Per the U.S. State Department website, examples of nonimmigrant classes of admission include foreign government officials, temporary visitors for business and pleasure, aliens in transit, academic and vocational students.

Unlike people granted "green card" status, who may live in the United States essentially without restrictions, nonimmigrants are only authorized to enter the country for specific purposes. Nonimmigrants' duration of stay and lawful activities, such as employment, travel, and accompaniment by dependents, are prescribed by their class of admission. No matter what country a nonimmigrant comes from, the purpose of their intended travel and other factors will determine what type of visa is required for them to enter the United States under U.S. immigration law.

Ambassadors and their families travel on passports issued to them by their home country and are issued *diplomatic visas* from the U.S. Department of State, category A. Foreign military personnel stationed in the United States are issued "official use only" passports by their home country and are issued visas from the U.S. Department of State, category A-1.

From the U.S. State Department website for Categories of Visas: Generally, a citizen of a foreign country who wishes to enter the United States must first obtain a visa, either a nonimmigrant visa for temporary stay, or an immigrant visa for permanent residence[5]. You must have a student visa to study in the United States. Your course of study and the type of school you plan to attend determine whether you need an F visa or an M visa.

To enter the United States to attend:	You need the following visa category:
University or college	
High School	F
Private elementary school	

Students of a foreign country who wish to enter the United States to study are issued passports by their home country, and are issued nonimmigrant visas from the U.S. Department of State, category F. See above.

Senator John McCain's parents were not immigrants to Panama, but if he wasn't eligible why didn't Senator Barack Obama sue to disqualify him? Barack Obama was likely terrified of the discovery phase of any trial where he would have had to provide documentation that showed his Kenyan father was a nonimmigrant, a student of a foreign country who temporarily entered the United States to study. Barack Obama, Senior was issued a passport by his home country of Kenya and was issued a visa from the U.S. Department of State, category F. In the discovery phase it would have been clear to judges and juries that Senator Barack Obama II was not a "natural born citizen;" that he wasn't born to American *parents*.

That should have been the end of it. But it wasn't.

CHAPTER 10
DEMOCRAT PRESIDENTIAL NOMINEE SENATOR BARACK OBAMA

Senator Barack Obama's[1] eligibility to hold the Office of the President was discussed at length during the campaign by different entities and for different reasons. His disqualifying factors, which were evident in law and should have been made known to the American public, weren't discussed. The media focused on the fact he was born in Hawaii. They pounded the table to emphasize their point.

With the help of Hollywood, the Democrats and the media started a disinformation campaign of propaganda assuring Americans that simply being born in the U.S. made Barack Obama a "natural born citizen." This was the BIG LIE. Americans relied on the media for accurate answers. Their refrain was that Obama was born in Hawaii and *that alone* made him a "natural born citizen." When repeated across the country thousands of times a day, this was reinforcing propaganda. The media did not report that Senator Obama was born of an American mother and a nonimmigrant foreign national holding a Kenya passport with a State Department-issued student visa F who had to return to Kenya and his family at the completion of his studies in the U.S. These were facts, and the media would not give them up and report them willingly.

Neither did the media report that Barack Obama, Senior was already married when he married Stanley Ann Dunham. Researchers uncovered a May 19, 1962 letter from Barack Obama, Senior to a friend, Tom Mboya (location unknown) which references his first wife, Kezia (Aoko) Obama, whom he married in January 1957. There are no records that Barack Obama, Senior ever divorced her. In 1959, Obama, Senior departed Kenya for America, leaving Kezia behind. She was three months pregnant with their daughter Auma. Obama, Senior also left behind a year-old son, Roy, who had been born in March 1958.

In 1961, few people in the Foreign Student Advisor world of the university were willing to pursue a case of bigamy by a nonimmigrant foreign student. Barack Obama, Senior's action were considered unusual for a nonimmigrant on a student visa.

In 2008, to avoid greater complications, the media had to find an answer to the question: was their candidate a "natural born citizen," under either the concept of *jus sanguinis* or under the concept of *jus soli?* Confusing American *citizenship* with the requirement to serve as President of the United States, the media embarked on a disinformation campaign of "... Senator Obama was born in Hawaii to an American mother and that is sufficient to make him a 'natural born citizen' in the eyes of the Constitution."

The essence of propaganda consists in winning people over to an idea so sincerely, so vitally, that in the end they succumb to it utterly and can never escape from it.

–Joseph Goebbels

The Naturalization Act of 1790 stated, "*...the children of citizens of the United States*, that may be born beyond the sea or out of the limits of the United States, *shall be considered as natural born citizens*."

Simply being born in Hawaii to an American mother is *insufficient* to make him a "natural born citizen."

ELIGIBILITY FOR PRESIDENT OF THE USA

When the Father is a:	And the Mother is a: US Citizen	Foreign National
US Citizen	Natural Born Citizen	
Foreign National		

Was the constant harangue—a form of brainwashing? Was this an example of semantic satiation? Was the constant refrain of a lie—born in Hawaii to an American mother is sufficient to become a U.S. citizen but insufficient to make anyone a "natural born citizen"—to a nationwide audience designed to convince that audience that the source was sincere in their support of their candidate? Was this an advanced mind control technique from a dark psychology textbook? Absolutely.

Leon James, a professor of psychology at the University of Hawaii's College of Social Sciences, coined the term *semantic satiation* in 1962. In James's doctoral thesis at McGill University on the subject, he described a variety of experiments he had conducted to explore how the concept affects thinking.

"It's a kind of a fatigue," James says. "It's called *reactive inhibition*: When a brain cell fires, it takes more energy to fire the second time, and still more the third time, and finally the fourth time it won't even respond unless you wait a few seconds. So that kind of reactive inhibition that was known as an effect on brain cells is what attracted me to an idea that if you repeat a word, the meaning in the word keeps being repeated, and then it becomes refractory, or more resistant to being elicited again and again."

In other words, when you tell a partial lie or a lie that is positively *incredible* (as in the BIG LIE) and keep repeating it, people will get tired of the harangue. They begin to think it might be believable, and eventually they do believe it because they are tired of hearing about it over and over again. *It must be true....* The reason people believe the lie, according to psychologists who study such things, is because the mind gets tired of sorting out fact from fiction and actually gives up. *It must be true.... It must be true....*

As we continue, we'll fight *semantic satiation* and mind fatigue with facts. This is the essence of *counter-propaganda*. The best antidote to the shenanigans of the manipulators in the media are facts which are completely transparent, verifiable, and free.

Being born to an American mother makes the son, by definition of the citizenship laws of the United States[2] (and *jus sanguinis*) a citizen of the United States. Period. Full Stop. There are no records that suggest Barack

Obama II was anything but a citizen of the U.S. Even when his mother took him to Indonesia, as Barry Soetoro or Barack Obama, he likely remained a U.S. citizen. In our analysis, Stanley Ann Dunham ensured her son maintained his U.S. citizenship.

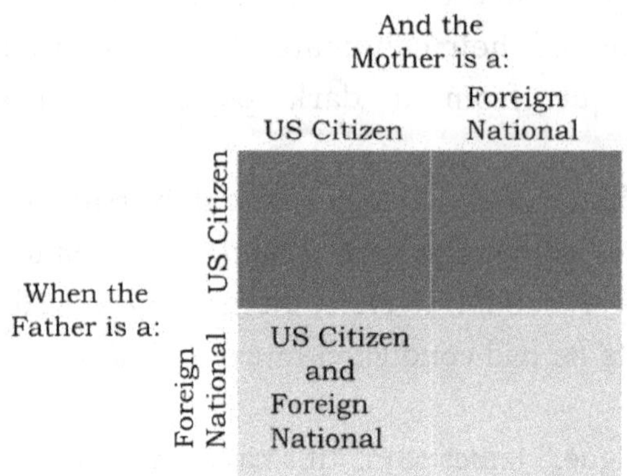

Second, Barack Obama was the son of a Kenyan father. Regardless of his father's immigration status or marital status, Kenyan law prevailed on its Kenyan citizens. Barack Obama, Senior held Kenya passport #84764. Being born to a nonimmigrant father who was a foreign national makes the son a citizen of his father's nationality by definition of the citizenship laws and the norms of his home country. Specifically, The Republic of Kenya Constitution[3], Chapter 3 Citizenship, Section 14—Citizenship by Birth, Item (1) states "A person is a citizen by birth if on the day of the person's birth, whether or not the person is born in Kenya, either the mother or father of the person is a citizen." Barack Obama, Senior, a Kenyan citizen, was subject to the jurisdiction of Kenyan law. Under the concept of nationality law, *jus sanguinis*, Barack Obama II was also a citizen of Kenya by birth. Kenyan law provides for the designation of dual nationals.

The U.S. has reciprocity agreements with foreign countries called bilateral agreements. Under the concept of reciprocity, the U.S. would have recognized the dual citizenship of Barack Obama II, upon his birth to a Kenyan national and a U.S. citizen.

This level of information is not immediately obvious, nor is it specifically articulated on a baby's identity document, i.e., birth certificate. Every nation has its own set of laws that govern the birth of a citizen child. A parent's basic personal factors (name, date of birth, place of birth) are required to *establish* a newborn's citizenship. Any other personal information (religion, immigration status, etc.) is incidental to the issuance of a birth certificate, but those and other incidentals may be required to comply with a foreign nation's immigration laws.

The place of birth is immaterial for a child who is a dual national. Because the child is a citizen of two countries, the immigration and naturalization laws of both countries must be followed if the child is to enjoy the full privilege of being a citizen of both countries. There is no "extra credit" for being born in one country over the other.

From the U.S. State Department[4], "Dual nationals owe allegiance to both the United States and the foreign country. They are required to obey the laws of both countries, and either country has the right to enforce its laws on them until such time as a person renounces their citizenship. It is important to note the problems attendant to dual nationality. Claims of other countries upon U.S. dual-nationals often place them in situations where their obligations to one country are in conflict with the laws of the other. In addition, their dual nationality may hamper efforts of the U.S. Government to provide consular protection to them when they are abroad, especially when they are in the country of their second nationality." There are travel advisories for those with dual citizenship. One such advisory states that if a dual national leaves the United States using a U.S. passport, then that traveler must use the same passport when returning to the U.S.

Natural born citizenship for a person born of one American and one alien parent may not have been resolved in the eyes of a law student, but what was resolved and indisputable was that a person "born of one American and one alien parent" was *concurrently* an American citizen *with citizenship in the other parent's country*. This is a person with two citizenships. A dual national[5].

The Republic of Kenya Constitution[6], Chapter 3 Citizenship, Section 16—Dual Citizenship states: "A citizen by birth does not lose citizenship by acquiring the citizenship of another country."

By Kenyan law, Barack Obama, Senior was required to register the birth of his son within 90 days of the live birth. Required documentary evidence of the birth may be a certificate of birth issued by the appropriate authority in the country abroad. By Kenyan law, residents abroad, and Barack Obama, Senior was a nonimmigrant studying abroad, "must complete Form BDA1[7] with a certified or notarized copy of the child's birth certificate."

CASE OF BARACK OBAMA

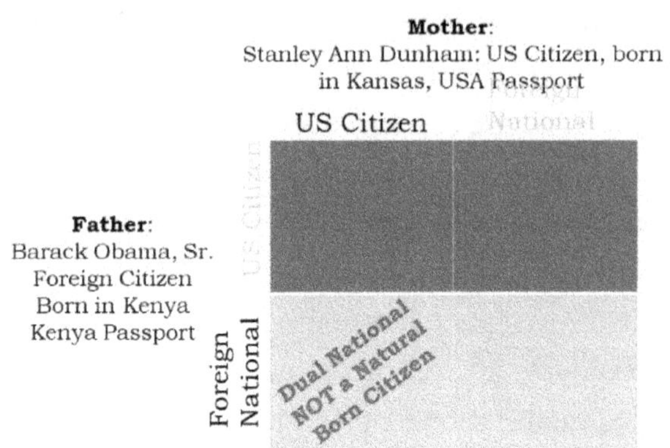

We assume all required paperwork to register the newborn son of Barack Obama, Senior and Stanley Ann Dunham was completed in a timely fashion. It was in the interest of the nonimmigrant father not to run afoul of the university's Foreign Student Advisor office or the Immigration & Naturalization Service. Stanley Ann Dunham also had responsibilities to perform with respect to their child because her husband was a nonimmigrant on a student visa. We will discuss those in an upcoming chapter.

These are the facts. If the Democrat party wanted any chance of winning the election with their chosen candidate, they would have to ignore the laws of two countries. The media did this with propaganda, as they claimed Barack Obama was a "natural born citizen" several times a day all across America. But no matter how many times they made that claim, one must ask the *counter-propagandist* question: "Where is the U.S. law that provides the son of a foreign national is a qualified 'natural born citizen?'" That answer is, "There isn't any such law."

We never believed that investigators from either political party were sent to Kenya to seek a copy of Barack Obama's birth certificate proving he was born in Kenya. However, investigators from both political parties could have been sent to Kenya to seek a certified or notarized copy of Barack Obama II's birth certificate *proving his Kenyan father registered Barack Obama II as a newborn Kenyan national* as required by Kenya law. (Emphasis added.)

Finding proof of that registration in a Nairobi or Mombasa immigration office would have been explosive. This would have been additional proof at the earliest stages of the campaign that Barack Obama II was a dual national with American and Kenyan citizenships, and was not a "natural born citizen" as the media and its surrogates claimed and chanted. It should now be obvious that any child of a Kenyan citizen is not eligible to hold the office of the President of the United States. But the unrelenting propaganda from the media made it difficult to know what to think.

It would not be impossible to prove with sufficient repetition and a psychological understanding of the people concerned that a square is in fact a circle. They are mere words, and words can be molded until they clothe ideas and disguise.
–Joseph Goebbels

The media and Democrat Party manufactured evidence by having a slate of lawyers state for the record that Barack Obama was a "natural born citizen." No official I&NS immigration attorney ever made that statement. The media did not report the facts, although they may have known them. There was no evidence to support their claims of eligibility. They pounded the table to distract the U.S. people, calling anyone who doubted them a racist.

This is opposite of what the Democrats did every day during President Clinton's impeachment hearings. They walked past the U.S. Capitol evidence room, never once going inside to see the evidence against President Clinton. This gave them deniability. The evidence was there; they refused to see it. Concerning Barack Obama's eligibility, they saw evidence that was not there. They shouted it from the rooftops, but mere noise cannot change facts. Incessantly repeating a verifiably factual falsehood still denies the law and the facts. These propaganda actions and activities were intended to create an "Illusion of Truth." Actually, an "Illusion of Legitimacy."

There is no finer example of the Goebbels's protocol—Tell a lie often enough and people will start to believe it. The media and the Democrat Party were counting on it. Uncle Joseph Goebbels' full quote on this issue is illuminating.

"If you tell a lie big enough and keep repeating it, people will eventually come to believe it. The lie can be maintained only for such time as the State can shield the people from the political, economic and/or military consequences of the lie. It thus becomes vitally important for the State to use all of its powers to repress dissent, for the truth is the mortal enemy of the lie, and thus by extension, the truth is the greatest enemy of the State."

–Joseph Goebbels

And this is what the American media and the Democrat Party did—use all of their powers to repress dissent and the lie. There comes a point when the lies catch up with those who pound the table.

Remember the good ol' boys of the 108th and 109th Congress who proposed amendments that would remove the wording disqualifying Obama from the U.S. Constitution. Recall the McCain Resolution, and when it was in the Democrat Party's power to "resolve" Obama's question of ineligibility with a Senate Resolution, they chose not to. Now remember Jill Pryor's 1988 law student article. Her example of "a person born of one American and one alien parent" was tailor-made to describe Barack Obama's particular situation. The media and politicians were well aware of her law school journal article. In the universe of law articles, hers is the only mention of "whether a person born of one American and one alien parent" could be a "natural born citizen" and that particular assertion hasn't been resolved.

Analysis of the raw statement "a person born of one American and one alien parent hasn't been resolved" is technically true in that no one has tried to make the case *in a court of law* that a dual national could be considered a "natural born citizen." Immigration law has already resolved and defined "a person born of one American and one alien parent" as a dual national, but to date, over two centuries after the signing, no one has brought a case to court that argues a new fault of the Constitution, a new discriminatory charge—the Constitution discriminates against *dual nationals* in determining presidential eligibility. Maybe James C. Ho, the author of *Unnatural Born Citizens and Acting Presidents*[8] could come up with a new article and argue that the Constitution discriminates against dual nationals since they can't be president.

We have the Constitution. We have seen the Immigration & Naturalization laws. We have read what the Founders were thinking. We know what their decisions were, and how they were codified in law. We have seen the references to the definition of a dual national as a person born of one American and one alien parent. That is the correct way to resolve an issue: look at all the facts and review all the related literature on the subject. Analyze the findings and draw a conclusion.

The strategy of the media and the Democrat Party was to propagandize the issue and repeat *ad nauseam*, "Barack Obama was born in Hawaii and is a natural born citizen." This was reverse engineering to achieve an outcome and not research. To create the illusion that Senator Obama was eligible to run for president they were willing to destroy Senator McCain, a veteran and a former prisoner of war by using cowardly insinuations, unfounded charges of racism, and as we see later in the campaign, even unfounded charges of Islamophobia.

This is a good place to discuss the September 2008 interview[9] between Mr. Stephanopoulos and Senator Obama. What follows is the actual transcript of that interview. Some have said Senator Obama admitted he was of the Muslim faith. We noticed something else in the interview.

Mr. Stephanopoulos: You mentioned your Christian faith. Yesterday you took after the Republicans for suggesting you have Muslim connections. Just a few minutes ago, Rick Davis, John McCain's campaign manager, said they've never done that. This is a false and a cynical attempt to play the victim.

Senator Obama: You know what, these guys love to throw a rock and hide their hands.

Mr. Stephanopoulos: But the McCain campaign has never suggested you have Muslim connections.

Senator Obama: No. No. No. But I don't think that when you look at what is being promulgated on Fox News, let's say, and Republican commentators who are closely allied to these folks...

Mr. Stephanopoulos: But John McCain said that's wrong.

Senator Obama: Listen, you and I both know that the minute that Governor Palin was forced to talk about her daughter, I immediately said that's off limits. And ...

Mr. Stephanopoulos: And John McCain said the same thing about questioning your faith.

Senator Obama: And what was the first thing the McCain campaign went out and did? They said, look, these liberal blogs that support Obama are out there attacking Governor Palin. Let's not play games. What I was suggesting—you're absolutely right that John McCain has not talked about my Muslim faith....

Mr. Stephanopoulos (interrupting): Your Christian faith.

Senator Obama: My Christian faith—well, what I'm saying is....

Mr. Stephanopoulos (interrupting): Connections, right.

Senator Obama: ...that he hasn't suggested that I'm a Muslim, and I think that his campaign upper echelons haven't either. What I think is fair to say is that coming out of the Republican camp, there have been efforts to suggest that perhaps I'm not what who I say I am when it comes to my faith, something which I find deeply offensive, and that has been going on for a pretty long time.

Next we have *Comments from Snopes* regarding the interview: A very brief, out-of-context segment was then clipped from that exchange and sent winging around the Internet as proof that Senator Obama had "admitted his Muslim faith," something even the right-leaning *Washington Times* acknowledged was false: But illustrating the difficulty of preventing false rumors about his faith from spreading, anti-Obama groups within one hour of the interview had sliced it out of context and were sending it around via email. They also were blogging about it.

We watched this interview several times before deciding that Obama seemed to want to blame McCain and his campaign for something not well defined. It was obvious that Obama wanted to play the victim; that he was geared up for it and came out of the blocks essentially declaring he was a victim, and McCain wasn't playing fair. The lifelong Democrat George Stephanopoulos was put in the unenviable position of defending Senator McCain with: "Rick Davis, John McCain's campaign manager, said they've never done that. This is a false and a cynical attempt to play the victim." *Playing the Victim* is one of the most well understood and easiest of the mind control techniques in *dark psychology*.

Obama *insinuated* no one should believe what Rick Davis may have said, and he kept insinuating that there was anti-Muslim, *Islamophobia* in the McCain campaign's staffers' hearts and minds. He was mockingly disgusted with McCain.

Mr. Stephanopoulos repeatedly came to McCain's defense. Senator Obama seemed to feel he was losing Stephanopoulos and the argument. He began to shoot from the hip with a blunderbuss, tangentially blaming Fox News and Republican commentators of Islamophobia, those people who were "closely allied to these folks...."

There was more *Analysis from Snopes:* Obama's remark that "...you're absolutely right that John McCain has not talked about my Muslim faith ..." was a straightforward statement: He was not "proclaiming" his "Muslim faith"; rather, he was acknowledging that Republican nominee John McCain had not specifically promulgated the false rumor that he (Obama) was a Muslim.

In the video, Senator Obama tried several times to make the case that the McCain campaign was suggesting Obama was a Muslim until he was forced to admit: "What I was suggesting—you're absolutely right that John McCain has not talked about my Muslim faith...."

George Stephanopoulos gave Senator Obama every opportunity to refute the implication that he was being portrayed as a Muslim. If the truth were a simple "no," then kill the rumor with facts, state some version of: "Jesus Christ is The Lord, I have been a member of the Church of Christ for 20 years, I was wed in the church and my children were baptized in the church—any attempt to tie me to Islam is a fool's errand and wrong." But Obama didn't say any of that. That is not how you use propaganda. Obama used the political tactic of shifting the blame onto McCain. This was propaganda. For the sake of this argument we put Obama's responses into a continuous stream of thought.

Notice the common *dark psychology* methods of *blame* and *avoidance*, methods of manipulating the conversation by not giving straight answers or by moving the discussion into a different topic using diversionary tactics:

"You know what, these guys love to throw a rock and hide their hands. No. No. No. But I don't think that when you look at what is being promulgated on Fox News, let's say, and Republican commentators who are closely allied to these folks.... Listen, you and I both know that the minute that Governor Palin was forced to talk about her daughter, I immediately said that's off limits. And ... what was the first thing the McCain campaign went out and did? They said, look, these liberal blogs that support Obama are out there attacking Governor Palin. Let's not play games. What I was suggesting—you're absolutely right that John McCain has not talked about my Muslim faith.... My Christian faith—well, what I'm saying is.... ...that he hasn't suggested that I'm a Muslim, and I think that his campaign upper echelons haven't either. What I think is fair to say is that coming out of the Republican camp, there have been efforts to suggest that perhaps I'm not what who I say I am when it comes to my faith, something which I find deeply offensive, and that has been going on for a pretty long time."

Notice how Senator Obama spends more time arguing against the implied charge of being a Muslim than was necessary to make the point. If it was a simple case of misunderstanding all that was needed was to look into the camera and declare, "No, I am not a Muslim. I am a Christian."

Instead he changes the topic of the conversation, pleading his case that he is being unfairly accused of being a Muslim, that he is the victim of some crime, that McCain's campaign was Islamophobic, that McCain and his campaign threw slam-grams, threw imaginary rocks at him, and called him names. It wasn't entirely obvious what Obama was trying to accomplish other than to paint McCain as an Islamophobe, but it seemed Stephanopoulos wasn't buying Obama's narrative nor the McCain-is-an-Islamophobe angle.

Where have we seen this strategy of attacking the messenger before? Remember an earlier obfuscation? Unable to answer the simple yes or no question, "Are you a 'natural born citizen," the American people got: "Look, I'm very clear-eyed about the fact that they are going to engage, as you said, in what they have done throughout this administration, which is just, let's just be very candid and straightforward, they're going to engage in lies, they're going to engage in deception, they're going to engage in an attempt to distract from the real issues that are impacting the American people[10]."

As we have pointed out, in *dark psychology* this is a method called, "Playing the Victim."

Let's review. There is a gross lack of credibility in hired attorneys uttering on cue and without evidence, "He is a natural born citizen," while ignoring the legal definition and its history. Contrast that with a future federal judge's assertion, "Whether a person born of one American and one alien parent, qualifies as natural born has never been resolved."

This is no difference when the media trots out someone they believe is a distinguished and revered journalist to badmouth a former president like CNN did when it put on Carl Bernstein to call President Trump a domestic war criminal[11].

The left, the media, and the Democrat Party ignored the definition of a dual national. They ignored the fact that it takes a foreign national to make a dual national and that Barack Obama's father was a *de facto* and legal foreign national. When Stanley Ann Dunham filed for divorce in January 1964, when Obama, Senior could not get a marriage-based green card, when the universities and the I&NS had enough of his shenanigans, he was deported back to Kenya.

DATE AND PORT OF LAST ARRIVAL IN UNITED STATES 8/9/59 NEW YORK
NAME OF VESSEL
PASSPORT NUMBER 84764
PASSPORT ISSUED BY (Name of Country) KENYA
PASSPORT EXPIRES ON 30th APRIL 1964
MARITAL STATUS MARRIED
IF MARRIED, GIVE NAME AND ADDRESS OF SPOUSE LEGAL SEPARATION ANN OBAMA, USC 2 MOS AGO
NAMES AND ADDRESSES OF CHILDREN c/o UNIV OF HAWAII HONOLULU HAWAII, BARACK OBAMA 2nd, 2 yrs USC
SOCIAL SECURITY NUMBER HAS ONE?
OCCUPATION STUDENT
(Insert "HAVE" or "HAVE NOT"): HAVE NOT BEEN EMPLOYED OR ENGAGED IN BUSINESS IN THE UNITED STATES.
IF YOU HAVE BEEN EMPLOYED OR ENGAGED IN BUSINESS IN THE UNITED STATES, GIVE THE FOLLOWING:

The I&NS and University of Hawaii records show Barack Obama, Senior, Kenya passport #84764, U.S. State Department-issued "nonimmigrant" student visa F, did everything possible to stay in the United States.

Questions of Senator John McCain's eligibility were a simple and transparent matter, easily understood and fully "resolved" by history and a politically inspired, yet bogus Senate resolution. It affirmed he was a "*natural born citizen*," but it also inserted the Democrat talking point—

which was wholly unnecessary, inaccurate, and propagandistic—that "*natural born citizen*" isn't defined anywhere in the Constitution.

Barack Obama, "a person born of one American and one alien parent," was a very straightforward case of an ineligible man running for the presidency. He should have been run off the stage. But the election of an illegitimate candidate suggests it wasn't a mistake of law (they tried to change the law to make Obama eligible) but a treacherous conspiracy and possible treason.

...for the truth is the mortal enemy of the lie, and thus by extension, the truth is the greatest enemy of the State.

-Joseph Goebbels

Why did they do it?

CHAPTER 11
IF IT WASN'T BRAINWASHING, THEN WHAT WAS IT?

The Democrats' daily drumbeat admonished Americans for listening to any Republican or Fox News. They insisted Americans listen to their media and Hollywood's greatest, because the Republicans were on a crusade with their far-right wing claims that Senator Obama was an ineligible candidate. They stated that everyone knows "natural born citizen" is not defined anywhere in the Constitution, and that Barack Obama was born in Hawaii to an American mother. They demanded Americans believe the ladies on *The* View, *The Ellen DeGeneres Show, Oprah,* or the dudes on *The Tonight Show* who had asserted that Republicans lie. They insisted the Democrats had shown all the evidence to make him eligible.

Remember this previously referenced bit of political theater from Senator Harris when she was queried if she was a "natural born citizen." She is on video saying, "Look, I'm very clear-eyed about the fact that they are going to engage, as you said, in what they have done throughout this administration, which is just, let's just be very candid and straightforward, they're going to engage in lies, they're going to engage in deception, they're going to engage in an attempt to distract from the real issues that are impacting the American people." And who can forget Senator Obama's own words of obfuscation on whether he was a Muslim: "You know what, these guys love to throw a rock and hide their hands. No. No. No. But I don't think that when you look at what is being promulgated on Fox News, let's say, and Republican commentators who are closely allied to these folks.... Listen, you and I both know that the minute that Governor Palin was forced to talk about her daughter, I immediately said that's off limits. And ... what was the first thing the McCain campaign went out and did? They said, look, these liberal blogs that support Obama are out there attacking Governor Palin. Let's not play games."

The goal was not only to play the victim but to also convince Americans that the far-right are liars and cheats, and the media and Democrat Party are lily-white, the Lone Rangers of the truth to be trusted above all others.

In *dark psychology* there are separate definitions for behavior modification, brainwashing, and *manipulation*. William Cooper, the author of *Dark Psychology and Manipulation*[1] describes manipulation as "a type of social influence aimed at changing the perception or behavior of others using linguistic tricks, devious schemes, subliminal and deceptive methods. Manipulation can be said to be aimed at the coarse reworking of elements, mostly for tendentious or fraudulent purposes." But more than that, "...the manipulator tries to lead the other towards his own ideas for personal gain and very special interests, and the manipulator can do this either by using sneaky manipulative techniques or by using extreme persuasion techniques. In any case, most of the tactics he will use will be deceptive and exploitative."

The Left uses this same manipulation trick to attack the Second Amendment. After every mass shooting, the prime-time network hosts or their on-call subject matter experts decry, "Who needs an AR-15 (or an assault weapon) to hunt deer?" Before any investigation into the shooting, the media or Democrats rush to a microphone and shriek something to the effect that "...Republicans are defending (Democrat-defined terms) assault weapons or weapons of war!" Then they utter the obligatory statements about banning private ownership of weapons, repealing the Second Amendment, or implementing more gun control. The Second Amendment actually states: *A well-regulated militia, being necessary to the security of a free people, the right of the people to keep and bear arms shall not be infringed.*

The Democrats want to reshape the meaning and applicability of the Second Amendment with indignant cries about the horrors of mass shootings and the needless use of an AR-15 to hunt deer. This is an attempt to manipulate Americans to see the Second Amendment, not as a constitutional right to self-protection, but as a more mundane or arbitrary rule about gun use in hunting. The Second Amendment has nothing to do with hunting but has everything to do with the right under the Constitution to protect oneself against a hostile government or entity.

There are hundreds of U.S. Supreme Court cases regarding the First and Second Amendments. For more than a hundred years the Democrat Party has sought increasingly greater control of guns and speech. Their ultimate goal is abolishing the right to keep and bear arms and abolishing the right to free speech. These are the activities of a totalitarian; these are the goals of a domestic enemy.

Newsflash: the media and the Democrat Party engaged in raw propaganda using these same manipulation, insinuation, and persuasion techniques every time they articulated their focus-group tested line, "Natural born citizen is not defined anywhere in the Constitution." It is a carefully crafted *insinuation* for the sole purpose of confusing the reader or the listener so that the people begin to question the veracity of the Constitution. Some of the media who associate with political figures become *master manipulators*, a term described in *dark psychology*.

The book *The Manchurian Candidate*[2] starts with a group of captured GIs who have terrible dreams. Their brains had been reprogrammed to respond to a certain stimulus: "What do you think of Sergeant Raymond Shaw?" Every time one of the captured soldiers was asked that specific question, they spouted the same Pavlovian response, "Raymond Shaw is the most bravest, kindest, warmest most wonderful human being I've ever known in my life."

Frank Sinatra, played the role of an Army major also robotically uttered those same words, "Raymond Shaw is the most bravest, kindest, warmest most wonderful human being I've ever known in my life." Speaking to a superior officer immediately afterwards, he confided, "At this moment I still feel that way, but in the back of my mind something tells me it's not true. It's just not true! It isn't as if Raymond is hard to like, he's impossible to like!!! In fact, he's probably one of the most repulsive human beings I've ever met in my whole life..."

The Raymond Shaw character in *The Manchurian* Candidate was programmed for a different response to a different stimulus, a phrase containing the word "solitaire," the card game. Now with all of the charm of a Walking Dead zombie, Raymond Shaw begins to robotically deal cards for a game of solitaire. When he turns over the queen of diamonds, he is immediately activated. Once activated, the former POW, Raymond Shaw, gazes straight ahead in a faraway stare and moves like an automaton to kill a political candidate. This movie demonstrates most American's understanding of brainwashing. It's not far from the standard definition.

Brainwashing is replacing a person's set of beliefs and ideas with the manipulator's chosen set of beliefs and ideas. In the brainwashing process there is a mechanism by which the victim is able to accept the change in programming which will lead to a change in behavior patterns. The easiest and most common behavior modification device used to achieve this shift in programming is violence or the threat of violence. Violence or the threat of violence can cause a person to accept a change in behavioral patterns quickly due to the fear of negative consequences. In *The Manchurian Candidate* brainwashing occurred when the GIs were subject to a series of negative consequences when they failed to comply with the manipulator's demands.

This is what the media did in the 2008 election. They *insisted* the American people believe Obama was a "natural born citizen" and the U.S. Constitution was faulty with their constant thrumming, "Natural born citizen is not defined anywhere in the Constitution!"

It took very little effort for the media to punish the Republican candidate or any Republican who would be voting for him. They used *power words, dramatic* insinuations or unfounded charges of racism or Islamophobia virtually every time the issue of Obama's eligibility was mentioned. These are subtle forms of violence. It is mental abuse at one end of the spectrum, manipulation at the far end of the other. Anyone who questioned Obama's birth certificate, for example, was verbally thrashed with charges of being a birther or other pejorative designed to inflict mental pain. Soon anyone with a simple question regarding Obama's eligibility was branded and stigmatized as a racist, birther, or Islamophobe. The victims learned to expect an attack whenever they asked a question about Obama. In the end, they stopped asking questions, and eventually only the manipulator's narrative was discussed.

Why does this happen? The defining factor in brainwashing is violence or threat of violence used to change the behavior of the *target*, in this case, anyone who was not going to vote for Barack Obama. The media told them, in so many words, "You're a racist if you don't vote for Barack Obama." No one wants to be labelled a racist. To keep the activists and protestors at bay, some people pulled the lever for Obama, the manipulator's desired behavioral outcome.

It happened countless times using guilt and propaganda. It may not have been mass brainwashing, but it was manipulation of the masses in its finest form. The repeated charge of racism or white supremacy turned a significant number of those who had been anti-Obama voters into reluctant Obama voters.

Remember the Frank Sinatra character in *The Manchurian Candidate*, uttering words that were actually being used against his will, "Raymond Shaw is the most bravest, kindest, warmest most wonderful human being I've ever known in my life." And recall what he said afterwards, "At this moment I still feel that way, but in the back of my mind something tells me it's not true. It's just not true! It isn't as if Raymond is hard to like, he's impossible to like!!! In fact, he's probably one of the most repulsive human beings I've ever met in my whole life..." The media's heavy-handed propaganda turned anti-Obama voters into saying, "...Obama is the kindest, warmest most wonderful human being I've ever known in my life and I will vote for him." And then afterwards, the person manipulated feels something like remorse, embarrassment, and mental anguish, "It's just not true! It isn't as if Obama is hard to like, he's impossible to like!!! In fact, he's probably one of the most repulsive human beings I've ever met in my whole life. Have you heard the crap that comes out of the so-called church that he attended for 20 years? He's a fraud, a vile racist, and a bigot, and plays the victim every time someone shoves a microphone in his face. I don't know why I say that now when I was sure, moments ago, that he was the kindest, warmest most wonderful human being I've ever known in my life." *Why is my brain doing that to me?*

Throughout society we are faced with negative consequences when we do something that transgresses societal norms. Criminals face negative consequences whenever they break the law. In these situations, the main purpose of brainwashing or programming is to create a *deterrent*. Break the law and you will be punished. Negative reinforcement seeks to punish unwanted or undesired behaviors. Manipulators steeped in *dark psychology* know through experience that *fear* is a much more effective tool than *praise*.

Not officially recognized as a product from the Nazi's Ministry of Propaganda, the CIA Office of Scientific Intelligence studied interrogation methods around 1951. Project ARTICHOKE[3] was a top secret mind control program whose purpose was to determine if a person could be made to involuntarily perform an act of *attempted* assassination. In 1959, the author of *The Manchurian Candidate*, Richard Condon, pushed the boundaries of what was thought to be secret research into an area of *dark psychology* with his interpretation of brainwashing by hostile forces. The goal of Project ARTICHOKE, *The Manchurian Candidate*, and the 2008 election was to get a target group to respond in a certain way through violence or the threat of violence. You can make the call whether the election was influenced from brainwashing by hostile media forces to stigmatization of being called a racist or an Islamophobe.

Project BLUEBIRD[4] focused on behavior modification experiments as a means of preventing Agency employees from providing intelligence to adversaries.

Operation MOCKINGBIRD[5] was an attempt to "manipulate the news media for propaganda purposes." From Wikipedia, according to author Deborah Davis, "Operation MOCKINGBIRD recruited leading American journalists into a propaganda network and influenced the operations of front groups. The CIA's support of these front groups was exposed when a 1967 *Ramparts* magazine article reported that the National Student Association received funding from the CIA. In 1975, Church Committee Congressional investigations revealed that in fact the Agency instigated and created connections with journalists and civic groups."

Also from the Wikipedia page, the Church Committee confirmed some earlier stories that charged the CIA with cultivating relationships with private institutions, including the press. Without identifying individuals by name, the Church Committee stated "...it found fifty journalists who had official, but secret, relationships with the CIA. In a 1977 *Rolling Stone* magazine article, 'The CIA and the Media[6],' reporter Carl Bernstein expanded upon the Church Committee's report saying around 400 press members were considered intelligence assets by the CIA, including *New York Times* publisher Arthur Hays Sulzberger, columnist and political analyst Stewart Alsop, and *Time* magazine. Bernstein documented the way in which overseas branches of major U.S. news agencies had for many years served as the 'eyes and ears' of Operation MOCKINGBIRD, which functioned to disseminate CIA propaganda through domestic U.S. media."

Secret mind control programs and brainwashing conducted by a hostile media and the U.S. government were happening in America. Who knew?

The mind control methods and procedures used by the media in 2008 were eerily similar to the special activities and research of foreign and domestic intelligence officers. As we have demonstrated, the media not only used mind control and behavior modification methods to silence a base of questioning voters, they also pressured them into voting for someone they did not want to vote for by using a version of the White/Black Model of propaganda: if you don't vote for Barack Obama you're a racist. They did this through various levels of perceived violence, mental anguish, or the threat of mental violence.

How does the White/Black Model of propaganda work? A reporter on television proposes two alternatives, painting them as the only ways out of a dilemma, one good and one bad. In our example, we had members of the media and Hollywood state emphatically, "If they are not going to vote for Barack Obama then they are racists." In this model, the trick is to propose that the other choice is so painful that people will have to follow the alternative.

This is the Illusion of Choice. There is no choice; you are being compelled to submit to their logic. To impress the horrors of racism on the mind, the debate on television centered on imagery of racism and more racism, at least in the background. Some people turned off the reporting, but those who remained focused on the television began to shift away from their previous position. Now they had doubts. They may not have had any racist thoughts, but they were not going to vote for Barack Obama. Maybe because he was hard on Israel or they had a bad feeling about the church he attended even if he was reportedly a Christian. But the reporters sowed doubt and created the illusion that the person running is a Christian and is just as qualified and eligible as any white person, so the voting came down to an issue of race. No one wants to be called a racist, under any circumstances, do they?

The leftist media and the Democrat Party are very knowledgeable and employ this method of behavior modification on their people. Democrats claim they are just as patriotic as the Republicans, citing the powerful imagery that Hitler used patriotism to make German people who were tired of war and humiliated by war into supporters of the Nationalist Socialist Worker's Party. Through Social Policy, many who did not want to be associated with the old school brand of patriotism warmed up to the idea of being part of a different group that was equally patriotic.

Then they repeated it over and over.

"The most brilliant propagandist technique will yield no success unless one fundamental principle is borne in mind constantly—it must confine itself to a few points and repeat them over and over."

-Joseph Goebbels

CHAPTER 12
DOMESTIC ENEMIES REQUIRE THEIR OWN MINISTRY OF PROPAGANDA

From 1934 to 1937, the Special Committee on Un-American Activities Authorized to Investigate Nazi Propaganda and Certain Other Propaganda Activities[1], held public and private hearings and collected testimony. Its mandate was to find how foreign subversive propaganda entered the U.S. and identify the organizations that were spreading it. Hollywood was at the top of the list to be investigated.

Hollywood stars, directors, and producers have become the latest version of Leni Riefenstahl[2], the German film director, photographer, and actress known for her role in producing Nazi propaganda. Like the Nazis exported propaganda to extol the virtues of Hitler, the promise of the Aryan race, the glories of fascism, the Democrat Party and the media used propaganda on the American people during the 2008 and 2012 elections to extol the virtues of Barack Obama, the promise of the African American race, and the glories of diversity. Democrats and the media labeled Republican candidates and voters as racists or white supremacists that leveraged white privilege against minorities.

Look on the web to find networks and newspapers that have been exposed for psychological operations they hid from American voters, such as: CNN Technical Director Admits the Network Was Pushing Propaganda with Fake Stories[3] and Behind the Curtain: How NYT Manufactures Lies For Democrats To Attack Their Opponents[4]. There are countless others.

Resolving issues of constitutional eligibility is not the responsibility of the media, Hollywood, or the Democrat Party. It is the purview of Congress or the Courts, and possibly the Federal Election Commission. Ignoring everything else, McCain received a unanimous Senate resolution; Obama's political party would not ever consider a Senate resolution. He wasn't eligible, and everyone knew it. His friends in the DNC tried to fix it for him but failed. Now they had to rely on the media to make him look like a legitimate candidate. When that failed, the media resorted to propaganda and the runes and bones of *dark psychology*.

McCain was continually attacked by the media and Democrats, but he didn't fight back adequately. The media tried to destroy McCain with innuendo and racist propaganda; the media gave Obama a pass. McCain was eligible; Obama was not. John McCain lost; Barack Obama became president.

Dark psychology works. Propaganda works.

According to his two autobiographies, Barack Obama was born in 1961 in Hawaii of a Kenyan father and an American mother. Opposition research conducted by members of his own party questioned his eligibility to hold the Office of President and determined him to be ineligible. Those conducting opposition research uncovered marketing materials which proclaimed Barack Obama had been "...born in Kenya, raised in Indonesia and Hawaii."

A publisher's standard procedure in developing marketing materials is for authors to provide detailed personal information, for example, providing biographies, citing previous works, including photographs, etc. Authors may include synopses, tag lines, previous awards and book reviews as well as other items of interest. When a publisher develops front and back cover work and other marketing materials, authors or aspiring authors provide pre-publication personal information and the author personally approves those materials before they go to print.

While the pamphlet for *Journeys in Black and White* and the claim that Obama had been born in Kenya was a distraction for the Obama campaign, Barack Obama's political profile increased with a good primary showing in South Carolina. The media was forced to take more notice. Their discovery of potentially adverse, possibly politically-disqualifying information should have placed the candidacy of Barack Obama under a microscope. *He just said he was born in Kenya!*

Barack Obama

Barack Obama, the first African American president of the Harvard Law Review, was born in Kenya and raised in Indonesia and Hawaii. The son of an American anthropologist and a Kenyan finance minister, he attended Columbia University and worked as a financial journalist and editor for Business International Corporation. He served as project coordinator in Harlem for the New York Public Interest Research Group, and was Executive Director of the Developing Communities Project in Chicago's South Side. His commitment to social and racial issues will be evident in his first book, *Journeys in Black and White*.

Barack Obama marketing material for *Journeys in Black and White*

Before we go any further, this is a good time to finish the discussion on Barack Obama's birth certificate.

Donald Trump credits himself with getting President Obama to release his birth certificate. After this release many articles and books were written which described Barack Obama's birth certificate as a forgery, some citing the marketing materials (from a book that was never written).

A "bait and switch" tactic is outlined in virtually every volume of *dark psychology* but we do not think that is what happened here. In the classic bait and switch tactic, the manipulator knows they have something the other side wants, perhaps a certificate of live birth from 1961. The manipulators in the media focused on the name of the hospital on the document and not the nationality of the father. Anyone realizing that

Barack Obama, Senior's Kenyan nationality disqualified Barack Obama II's quest for the office of the president was systematically vilified, ostracized, and stigmatized.

The manipulator's goal was for the investigators to look at something else, in this case, scrutinize the header. The bait was the name of the hospital on a certificate of live birth. The manipulator (the media) kept the investigators focused on the place of birth so they didn't look further into Obama's eligibility to be president. His father's obvious Kenyan citizenship was the switch. For political reasons that was never mentioned and neither was Obama's middle name as previously discussed.

Politics is a blood sport, a "...continuation of war by other means." (Clausewitz, *On War*). Some political opponents who were not fans of the junior senator from Illinois began a careful investigation of Barack Obama's history. They scrutinized the senator's two autobiographies, visited his State Senate office, and visited his church. They discovered Nation of Islam members reportedly had served on his staff in the Illinois Senate and the U.S. Senate. After Obama's DNC convention appearance, a reporter covering the Illinois senator attended Barack Obama's church, Chicago's Trinity United Church of Christ. She was very surprised to find Nation of Islam materials in the church's bookstore. *That* was a revelation. Some reporters moved to dismiss the finding as nothing. But to a counterterrorism specialist, this was actual evidence that strongly suggested Chicago's Trinity United Church of Christ may have been a front for the Nation of Islam. Noteworthy, the church didn't have any other church's materials for sale. Wikipedia describes that the Nation of Islam beliefs draw heavily on both Christianity and Islam, although the Nation of Islam interprets their sacred scriptures in ways different from Christians or mainstream Muslims[5]. The Nation of Islam has a presence abroad, with membership open to people of color but not whites.

Republican candidates for president watched the Obama witch trials—Democrats fighting Democrats—with amusement. Was he born in Hawaii, as he asserted in his autobiographies? Or was he born in Kenya as stated in the marketing materials that he *provided*? Suddenly investigators began asking real uncomfortable questions. Did he use that line to get priority placement at the university? Who paid for these expensive universities?

On the surface, this was a very minor issue. In 1991, Barack Obama said on his Acton & Dystel questionnaire for the potential book *Journeys in Black and White,* that he was born in Kenya. Kenya was a much more interesting location than what a birth certificate and birth announcements in the newspapers had confirmed, that he was just another U.S. citizen born in Hawaii.

Remember it's 1991, he's 30 years old and single. He has just graduated Harvard Law School. Columbia University proudly claimed Obama graduated in 1983[6]. Who is going to check him out? There is no reason for Acton & Dystel not to believe the questionnaire from their *Harvard grad*. It was also about this time—we are not 100% sure because of a paucity of records—that someone recognized the potential of Barack Obama II, not as an author but as a political candidate.

Like anyone with presidential aspirations, Barack Obama wrote an autobiography. *Dreams from my Father* was written in 2003 and published in 2004. In the same timeframe several congressmen were trying to amend the U.S. Constitution for the three-term state senator (1997-2005) to be eligible to run for president.

Fast forward to his presidential candidacy and the unique issues swirling about him, such as his constitutional eligibility and his twenty-year association with Trinity United Church of Christ and the Reverend Jeremiah Wright. Reverend Wright's speeches from the pulpit were captured for posterity and were available in the Trinity United Church of Christ bookstore. Speeches from Louis Farrakhan were also available in the church's bookstore.

This small excerpt[7] is from one of Reverend Wright's sermons: "...it is that whites are incapable of making any valid judgment about human existence. The goal of black theology is the destruction of everything white, so that blacks can be liberated from alien gods. The god of black liberation will not be confused with a blood thirsty white idol. Black theology must show that the black god has nothing to do with a God worshiped in white churches whose primary purpose is to sanctify the racism of whites and to daub the wounds of blacks."

Counterterrorism specialists studying the mechanics and dynamics of *dars* and *madrassas*, the Islamic girls' and boys' schools, have seen these (Reverend Wright and Farrakhan-like) sermons before. In the *madrassas* and mosques across the Middle East and Africa there is repetition of "the blame game," blame Israel, blame America, blame Christians, blame white people, and so on. Master manipulators shift the blame from one group to another, as repetition turns into propaganda and radicalization takes place. The Global Network on Extremism and Technology[8] offers some insight on how individuals within a society are radicalized. This accounting, is sadly representative of what is seen in the Muslim world that leverages propaganda, encourages adherents to be *juramentados* or 9/11 hijackers or worse.

We see the same proselytizing techniques employed in Reverend Wright's and Reverend Farrakhan's sermons; simply replace the words. White becomes *infidel* and black becomes *Muslim* for an understanding of what is inculcated in the *madrassas* and mosques. Make no mistake, this education through sermons is also a *dark psychology* technique. These are brainwashing tactics at their finest that result in near-total compliance to the speaker's world view.

By his own admission in his autobiographies, Barack Obama was a messed-up person before he attended Reverend Wright's church. Afterwards, he found purpose and discipline.

Here's a question to ponder, what kind of person would catch an al-Qaeda recruiter's eye? A Muslim Brotherhood recruiter?

When Senator Obama won the South Carolina primary, klaxons sounded within the Democratic National Committee and mainstream media establishment. It also woke up the other Democrats running for office. This had all the makings of a story of historic proportions. Prior to running for president in 2008, Senator Joe Biden said of his friend, Senator Barack Obama, "I mean, you got the first mainstream African-American who is articulate and bright and clean and a nice-looking guy. I mean, that's a storybook, man." The media dismissed Joe Biden's racist comments because he was a Democrat

The media likely ignored the previous congressional attempts to amend the Constitution, yet they quickly determined that the first African-American man who had a legitimate shot of being elected president had significant credibility and constitutional eligibility issues. He presented a certifiable dichotomy. If Senator Obama had been born in America, then presenting a certified Hawaiian birth certificate would kill the rumors that he may have been born in Kenya. But presenting his birth certificate would confirm what the media refused to report, that the junior senator from Illinois was the child of an American mother and a Muslim father who was a foreign national. The media knew the rules and the constitutional requirements for president. While seemingly perfect presidential candidate material, the real money-shot question "Was he eligible?"

However, if America found out that Senator Obama had lied about his birthplace in Hawaii and was actually "...born in Kenya, raised in Indonesia and Hawaii," as the 1991 marketing materials from Acton & Dystel seemed to suggest, the fallout would have been immediate disqualification of "the first mainstream African-American who is articulate and bright and clean...." After the September 11, 2001 attacks on America, the only thing that could have been worse would be discovering Barack Obama was a Muslim. Yes, he had a Muslim middle name but after 9/11, a significant size of the population thought that that was not something to be proud of.

Any documentation relating to Barack Obama's birth, citizenship, religion, or dual nationality would have destroyed any claim of being a "natural born citizen" and his candidacy for the presidency. And the media quietly put a moratorium on mentioning his Muslim middle name, as did John McCain and his campaign.

For whatever reason, someone in the Democrat party hierarchy, and someone at the very top level of the media conglomerates determined that they liked the cut of Obama's jib and still wanted him to be their candidate. (At this point you can almost hear Hillary scratching the side of the boat as she is dumped over the side.) He wasn't ready and would need work, but the media have all sorts of capabilities. Let the "Illusion of Truth" begin; release the hounds of obfuscation, distortion, and prevarication. Goebbels would have been so impressed. The Democrat Party and the media should have been wearing armbands and marching to the drums of "*Die Wacht am Rhein*," *The Watch on the Rhine*.

Presidential candidate Obama refused to answer the questions surrounding his eligibility and place of birth. He did not submit a birth certificate as proof of his bona fides during the campaign. (It wasn't until 2012 that the president released a certificate of live birth from Hawaii.) In performing the Chicago version of Muhammad Ali's "rope-a-dope" it seemed the media's chosen candidate had checkmated himself. There was little Senator Obama could do to extricate himself from the history he had created. He was in a box of his own making and needed help, the type of help only the media could provide.

The media could have dropped Barack Obama like a hot rock, but they chose to do something dramatic. The media and the Democrat Party genuflected, and minorities in Hollywood came to the aid of Senator Obama with a common theme: he was born in Hawaii, he is eligible, and it is racist to criticize an African American man. But above all, there will be no references to Islam or his father.

The media invested heavily in keeping Obama's eligibility issues and personal history off the nightly cable news networks. They focused on political and social issues, and ignored every aspect of the man's personal life as detailed in his autobiographies: his drug use, his affinity for a communist mentor, his relationship with the Reverend Jeremiah Wright and Chicago radicals. Any one of these issues would have derailed a Republican candidate's campaign train, but the left's propaganda measures were making a difference. Conservative media and Republicans watched the liberal senator with interest. He should have foundered under a crushing wave of suspicion and one political gaffe after another, the hallmarks of someone not up for the job. The media's propaganda emphasized that Obama identified as African American. Democrats are masters at exploiting racial sensitivities, real or imagined. Conservative media and Republicans had been outplayed.

Republicans were surprised by the rise in the polls of the ineligible candidate and did not have an answer for him. Some rushed to sue the Democrat candidate only to be rebuffed for not having any legal standing. Republicans were very sensitive about criticizing an African American in public, especially one with possible Islamic connections. The DNC knew it, and the media knew it. The left had been seeking a wedge issue to divide the Republican Party; now they had it. Keep McCain on his heels with charges of racism and ensure he doesn't mention Obama's middle name. The media played along.

The other Democratic presidential candidates sensed there could be a tidal shift in their election fortunes if the rising political star, Barack

Obama, could be exposed as a fraud for lying to a publisher to score literary points. If his campaign collapsed, he would have done it to himself. He performed incredibly well in front of a crowd, he looked fantastic in a suit, and he was the master of the teleprompter. But his Achilles heel was his history and documents, especially documents. Not those certificates which would attest to his birthplace, but silly publisher's catalogs and derogatory immigration documents from the U.S. and Kenya. The key to it all was the documented history of Barack Obama, Senior: a nonimmigrant, a student, and a citizen of Kenya which would also prove the son was a Kenyan citizen at birth. By Kenyan law, Barack Hussein Obama II was a dual national at birth, he was the son of a Kenyan national, and clearly wasn't eligible to the office of the U.S. president.

The media declared war on Republicans, and then the Democrats followed. The new media standard and propaganda tactic became anyone who questioned the legitimacy of the candidacy of Barack Obama in any form would be censored and then attacked. The quickest way would be to accuse the accusers of being racist and hammer that message home. Barack Obama's strong showing in South Carolina demonstrated that the media could use their mighty power to ignore issues of eligibility with great effect by playing what has become known as *the race card*.

If one is losing an argument in politics but is a racial minority, playing the race card gains one an instant political advantage. It shifts the focus from the issue under discussion to the topic of race. In *dark psychology*, this is called *deflection*.

When the Democrats played the race card on the McCain candidacy, it destroyed the Republican candidate. The Democrats were beginning to understand just how powerful racial propaganda could be. McCain could have had a chance to win the White House if he had taken the junior senator from Illinois to court. Our analysis is that McCain felt checkmated; he didn't want or deserve to be branded a racist. He couldn't criticize the African American candidate for fear of alienating the African American vote. There would be no fighting back from the former POW who proudly considered himself to be a *maverick*.

The media and the Obama campaign found the race card to be a useful propaganda tool. Throughout the presidential primaries, journalists and the TV networks downplayed the meaning of constitutional eligibility.

They deflected that issue and portrayed Senator Obama as the victim of racism whenever any a question of his credentials were raised. Barack Obama played the aggrieved victim to the hilt.

CHAPTER 13
BARACK OBAMA, SENIOR

Let us recall: A U.S. citizen is subject to the jurisdiction of the laws of the United States.

The media and Democrat Party would like America to close her eyes and plug her ears, starting now: A citizen of Kenya is subject to the jurisdiction of the laws of Kenya. During the election of 2008, this bit of trivia was actually *proscribed* news by the U.S. media And when it wasn't outlawed in newsrooms and networks, it was ignored.

One of the most insidious powers the media possesses is the power to ignore.
–Chris Plante

Let's investigate further, remembering the person of interest is Barack Obama, Senior. This information is relevant to understanding the full story, but it has not been discussed and is not widely known. Also know that the process for a foreign student to enter the United States hasn't appreciably changed since the 1950s. If anything, entry into the U.S. after September 11, 2001 has gotten more difficult. Even after 70 years, the basics and the forms for entering the United States are pretty much the same today as they were when Barack Obama, Senior sought to come to America.

From the Department of State's website[1], "a citizen of a foreign country who wishes to enter the United States must first obtain a visa, either a nonimmigrant visa for temporary stay, or an immigrant visa for permanent residence." In order for Barack Obama, Senior (before he became a "Senior") to study in the United States he needed a student visa. The course of study and the type of school Barack Obama, Senior planned to attend determined he needed an F visa, for academic studies, not vocational studies.

The policies, procedures, and laws that were the jurisdiction of the Immigration and Naturalization Service of the Department of Justice in the 1950s and 1960s are now under the purview of the U.S. Customs and Border Protection[2]. They assert on their website: "The United States supports international education and welcomes foreign students and exchange visitors. Students and exchange visitors must be accepted by their schools or program sponsors before applying for a nonimmigrant visa."

Barack Obama, Senior, a citizen of a foreign country—Kenya—wished to study in the United States. He applied to the Department of State for a nonimmigrant visa. Barack Obama, Senior was issued a Kenyan passport, #84764[3]. He was allowed entry into the U.S. as a nonimmigrant, and granted a student visa, Category F. Nonimmigrant classes[4] of admission include foreign government officials, temporary visitors for business and pleasure, *academic students*, and others. Nonimmigrants' duration of stay and lawful activities, such as attending college or university, employment, travel, and accompaniment by dependents, are prescribed by their class of admission.

Barack Obama, Senior attended a required interview by a State Department official.

The State Department advises foreign students on how to prepare for the required interview[5] by a State Department official.

Gather and prepare the following required documents before your visa interview:

Passport valid for travel to the United States.

Nonimmigrant Visa Application, Form DS-160 confirmation page.

Application fee payment receipt.

Photograph.

Certificate of Eligibility for Nonimmigrant (F-1) Student Status-For Academic and Language Students, Form I-20.

We can surmise Barack Obama, Senior successfully passed the visa interview and that he had all the required documents to travel to the U.S. He was issued a Nonimmigrant (F-1) Student visa and travelled to the United States.

An April 1961 internal "Memo for File" at the Immigration and Naturalization Service, documents that Mrs. McCabe, Foreign Student Advisor at the University of Hawaii, stated that Barack Obama, Senior's marriage to Stanley Ann Dunham had been reported to University of Hawaii officials. It also takes note of "Barack Obama's bigamy." The reference for the "Memo for File," written by I&NS official Lyle H. Dahlin, is sourced from an American Thinker article by Nick Chase of July 7, 2012 and titled Were Ann Dunham and Barack Obama Really Married?[6].

The "Memo for File" reads: "Mrs. McCabe at the University of Hawaii, Foreign Student Advisor, called on 4/10/61 and reported that BARACK H. OBAMA, a student at the University since 1959 was married on February 2, 1961 to Stanley Ann Dunham, a United States citizen from Seattle, Washington in Maui, Hawaii. The problem is that when he arrived in the U.S. the Subject had a wife in Kenya."

"The Subject was born on June 18, 1934 in Kisuru, Nyansa, Kenya, Africa and entered the U.S. at New York, N.Y. on August 9, 1959 as an F student. He has received an extension to stay to until August 8, 1961 and has received permission to accept employment up to 25 hours per week. He apparently is a bona-fide student and Mrs. McCabe states he is very intelligent."

"Mrs. McCabe further states that Subject has been running around with several girls since he first arrived here and last summer she cautioned him about his playboy ways. Subject replied he would 'try' to stayaway [sic] from the girls."

Three lines are redacted from the copy. The memo then continues: "Subject told Mrs. McCabe that in Kenya all that is necessary to be divorced is to tell the wife that she is divorced and that constitutes a legal divorce. Subject claims to have been divorced from his wife in Kenya in this method."

"Polygamy is not an excludable or (unreadable; may have been overstriked to indicate 'delete') or deportation charge as Subject is a non-immigrant and this is waived under 212(4). If he were convicted of bigamy we might get a deportation charge but not before. Subject is a bona-fide student at present. Recommend that Subject be closely questioned before another extension is granted—and denial be considered. If his USC wife tries to petition for him make sure an investigation is conducted as to the bona-fide of the marriage."

Three things to note from the I&NS Memo: Obama Senior had a wife in Kenya; I&NS official Lyle H. Dahlin referred to "his USC wife," as in Obama's U.S. *citizen* wife (Stanley Ann Dunham) who may try "to petition for him;" and Dahlin recommends "an investigation is conducted as to the bona-fide of the marriage." I&NS official Lyle H. Dahlin was referencing that a U.S. citizen spouse may petition the Department of State for a change of status for her husband from a nonimmigrant student visa F to an IR-1 immigrant visa.

Barack Obama, Senior *was not an immigrant*, he was a *nonimmigrant* with a student visa category F. This visa granted him admittance to the U.S. only for the duration of his student program with some additional months to gain work experience. After that, Barack Obama, Senior would have to return to his home country.

Like most African men on a nonimmigrant visa, after marrying Stanley Ann Dunham Barack Obama, Senior likely sought a change of status from nonimmigrant student F to immigrant IR-1. But getting married to a citizen doesn't automatically guarantee a change of status or a permanent stay for an international student. Certain requirements must be met before a green card can be obtained.

There is no evidence Barack Obama, Senior ever received a green card based on his marriage to Stanley Ann Dunham. Barack Obama II has repeatedly stated that his father met his mother in 1960 while he was studying at the University of Hawaii on a scholarship. They married in early 1961 and Stanley Ann Dunham gave birth to the younger Obama later that year. Barack Obama II revealed that his father left him and his mother when he was just two years old. He does not acknowledge that his father was living in Massachusetts with another woman while the elder Obama attended Harvard. There has never been any mention from the Junior Obama that Barack Obama, Senior had been denied an extension of his student visa in July 1964 and was deported back to Kenya, also in July 1964. The fact that Barack Obama, Senior was deported is overwhelming evidence he never received a green card and he never became a naturalized citizen.

CHAPTER 14
WHEN THEORY BECOMES A CONSPIRACY

Away from the bright lights of the media, the political parties are in a constant struggle to pass beneficial laws or void laws detrimental to the party in power. In 2003, Democrat Rep. Vic Snyder of the 108th Congress introduced H.J.R 59 which would have removed the "natural born citizen" requirement for president under Article II of the U.S. Constitution, and would have made a person who has been a citizen of the United States for at least 35 years and who has been a resident within the United States for at least 14 years eligible to hold the office of President or Vice President.

There was no reason for Rep. Vic Snyder and the other members of Congress to bombard the U.S. Congress in an effort to amend the U.S. Constitution other than to benefit an upcoming potential candidate—who wasn't a natural born citizen—for president.

In 2021, it may be difficult to comprehend that Democrats in 2003 had actually identified one of their members for executive-level positions (from state senator to U.S. Senator) and began grooming him for the office of the President. Barack Obama II might have made his presidential aspirations known which probably triggered the rush to amend the Constitution. *I'd like to run for president, but I have this eligibility problem....*

When the Democratic National Committee conducted a background investigation on the Illinois senator, Barack Obama II, they found he had issues, and his former membership in the Choom Gang was the least of their worries. Graduating from candidate to nominee pushed the nominee into the realm of state election laws and official documents.

As a two-time member of the U.S. Electoral College, Paul R. Hollrah was intimately aware of the process for selecting a president and vice president, and he was intimately knowledgeable of the official documents required to select a president and vice president. He stated there were three vetting opportunities, all involving documents:

"The first occurs immediately following the nominating conventions when the parties certify their candidates to the state election boards so that ballots can be printed." In the case of the Republicans, all of the required documents were provided to the fifty state election boards by the

Republican National Committee in 2008, and contained, verbatim, the following affirmation:

CERTIFICATE OF NOMINATIONS

State of Tennessee:

We do hereby certify that at a National Convention of Delegates representing the Republican Party of the United States, duly held and convened in the City of Saint Paul, State of Minnesota, on September 4, 2008, the following person, meeting the constitutional requirements for the Office of President of the United States, and the following person, meeting the constitutional requirements for the Office of Vice President of the United States, were nominated for such offices to be filled at the ensuing general election, November 4, 2008, viz.:

[illegible]	[illegible]	[illegible]	[illegible]
President of the United States	JOHN McCAIN	Republican	2211 East Camelback Road Phoenix, Arizona 85016
Vice President of the United States	SARAH PALIN	Republican	1140 West Parks Highway Wasilla, Alaska 99654

IN TESTIMONY WHEREOF, we have hereunto set our hand this 4th day of September, 2008

Permanent Address of Chairman of Convention } John A. Boehner, 7371 Charter Cup Lane, West Chester, OH 45069

John A. Boehner
Chairman of the 2008 Republican National Convention

Permanent Address of Secretary of Convention } Jean A. Inman, 437 Central Street, Avon, MA 02322

Jean A. Inman
Secretary of the 2008 Republican National Convention

John A. Boehner, being duly sworn, says that he was the presiding officer of the Convention of Delegates mentioned and described in the foregoing certificate, and that the said Jean A. Inman was the secretary of such convention, and that said certificate and the statements therein contained are true to the best of his information and belief.

Subscribed and sworn to before me this 4th day of September, 2008

Notary Public
My Commission expires on the 31 day of 1 20 10

Jean A. Inman, being duly sworn, says that she was the secretary of the Convention of Delegates mentioned and described in the foregoing certificate, and that the said John A. Boehner was the presiding officer of such convention, and that said certificate and the statements therein contained are true to the best of her information and belief.

Subscribed and sworn to before me this 4th day of September, 2008

Notary Public
My Commission expires on the 31 day of 1 20 10

"We do hereby certify that (at) *a national convention of Delegates representing the Republican Party of the United States, duly held and convened in the city of Saint Paul, State of Minnesota, on September 4, 2008, the following person, meeting the constitutional requirements for the Office of President of the United States, and the following person, meeting the constitutional requirements for the Office of Vice President of the United States, were nominated for such offices to be filled at the ensuing general election, November 4, 2008, viz;"* The documents contained the names and home addresses of John McCain and Sarah Palin, and were signed by John A. Boehner and Jean A. Inman, Chairman and Secretary, respectively, of the 2008 Republican National Convention, and notarized by Sheila A. Motzko. Attached is a copy of the Certificate of Nominations for Tennessee:

However, certifications provided to the state election boards by the Democratic National Committee were anything but uniform. This is what was submitted to state election officials in Hawaii:

"THIS IS TO CERTIFY that at the National Convention of the Democrat Party of the United States of America, held in Denver, Colorado on August 25 though (sic) *28, 2008, the following were duly nominated candidates of said Party for President and Vice President of the United States respectively and that the following candidates for President and Vice President of the United States are legally qualified to serve under the provisions of the United States Constitution."*

The other forty-nine states received the following certification:

"THIS IS TO CERTIFY that at the National Convention of the Democrat Party of the United States of America, held in Denver, Colorado on August 25 though (sic) *28, 2008, the following were duly nominated as candidates of said Party for President and Vice President of the United States respectively."*

The documents contained the names and home addresses of Barack Obama and Joe Biden. The document was signed by Nancy Pelosi and Alice Travis Germond, Chairman and Secretary, respectively, of the 2008 Democratic National Convention, and notarized by Shalifa A. Williamson.

Let's take a more in-depth look at these documents. Here they are in all of their glory. First what it is supposed to say; then what was actually submitted (with a received date stamp).

DEMOCRATIC NATIONAL COMMITTEE

OFFICIAL CERTIFICATION OF NOMINATION

THIS IS TO CERTIFY that at the National Convention of the Democratic Party of the United States of America, held in Denver, Colorado on August 25 though 28, 2008, the following were duly nominated as candidates of said Party for President and Vice President of the United States respectively and that the following candidates for President and Vice President of the United States are legally qualified to serve under the provisions of the United States Constitution:

For President of the United States

Barack Obama
5046 South Greenwood Avenue
Chicago, Illinois 60615

For Vice President of the United States

Joe Biden
1209 Barley Mill Road
Wilmington, Delaware 19807

Nancy Pelosi
Chair, Democratic National Convention

Alice Travis Germond
Secretary, Democratic National Convention

City and County of Denver)
) ss:
State of Colorado)

Subscribed and sworn to before me in the City and County of Denver, State of Colorado, this 28th day of August, 2008.

SHALIFA A. WILLIAMSON
Notary Public
State of Colorado
My Commission Expires September 06, 2011

Notary Public

September 6, 2011
Commission expiration date

Democratic Party Headquarters ■ 430 South Capitol Street, SE ■ Washington, DC 20003 ■ (202) 863-8000 ■ Fax (202) 863-8174
Paid for by the Democratic National Committee. Contributions to the Democratic National Committee are not tax deductible.
Visit our website at www.democrats.org.

What is noteworthy in the DNC documents of certification is that the phrase, "*... and that the following candidates for President and Vice President of the United States are legally qualified to serve under the provisions of the United States Constitution*" was omitted for 49 states.

Other than that, all of the documents were absolutely identical... even to the misspelling of the word "through" in the second line of the certifications.

DEMOCRATIC NATIONAL COMMITTEE

RECEIVED
AUG 29 2008
SC ELECTION COMM.

OFFICIAL CERTIFICATION OF NOMINATION

THIS IS TO CERTIFY that at the National Convention of the Democratic Party of the United States of America, held in Denver, Colorado on August 25 though 28, 2008, the following were duly nominated as candidates of said Party for President and Vice President of the United States respectively:

For President of the United States

Barack Obama
5046 South Greenwood Avenue
Chicago, Illinois 60615

For Vice President of the United States

Joe Biden
1209 Barley Mill Road
Wilmington, Delaware 19807

Nancy Pelosi
Nancy Pelosi
Chair, Democratic National Convention

Alice Travis Germond
Alice Travis Germond
Secretary, Democratic National Convention

City and County of Denver)
) ss:
State of Colorado)

Subscribed and sworn to before me in the City and County of Denver, State of Colorado, this 28 day of August, 2008.

SHALIFA A. WILLIAMSON
Notary Public
State of Colorado
My Commission Expires September 06, 2011

Shalifa A. Williamson
Notary Public

September 6, 2011
Commission expiration date

Democratic Party Headquarters ■ 430 South Capitol Street, SE ■ Washington, DC 20003 ■ (202) 863-8000 ■ Fax (202) 863-8174
Paid for by the Democratic National Committee. Contributions to the Democratic National Committee are not tax deductible.
Visit our website at www.democrats.org

This deceit was first reported by J.B. Williams in a September 10, 2009 article, titled, "The Theory is Now a Conspiracy and Facts Don't Lie[3]."

Immediately upon publication of Williams' article, Obama-doubters across the country began contacting their state election boards requesting copies of the Democrat and Republican Party candidate certifications. The full scale of the Democrats' deception was exposed.

If Barack Obama was 100% eligible and qualified per the media campaign, why would the DNC eliminate the language certifying that Obama and Biden were both eligible to serve "under provisions of the U.S. Constitution?" The only reasonable answer is what we already know. The Democrats could not honesty claim they didn't know he was not eligible to serve "under provisions of the U.S. Constitution." They actually knew in 2008 when they nominated him that Obama was ineligible to serve and that he was not a "natural born citizen." No one wanted to sign an obviously fraudulent document.

Barack Obama swore the following Goebbelsesque lie under penalty of perjury:

"I, the undersigned, do hereby solemnly swear or affirm that the abovementioned facts (his name and home address) *are true and correct and that I am fully qualified to become a candidate for the office of President of the United States and that I will be fully qualified to hold said office, if elected. I further swear or affirm that I have filed a statement of candidacy with the Federal Election Commission and have raised and expended not less than Five Thousand Dollars ($5,000.00) for said office."*

The J.B. Williams article, "The Theory is Now a Conspiracy and Facts Don't Lie" is a *tour de force* of journalism. It first reports how the Democrat Party illegally altered the state certification documents. Mr. Williams has the originals and the Democrat Party forgeries. He provided copies of each in his article. This is what conspiracy looks like.

When their lies are insufficient, Democrat politicians must rely on the media to lie for them and create an "Illusion of Truth," or in this case, an "Illusion of Legitimacy:" another version of "whatever is necessary truth," in lieu of "the truth, the whole truth, and nothing but the truth." This is the work the master manipulators, the DNC and media, did for Barack Obama.

Americans generally take for granted privileges that foreigners wish to possess, specifically U.S. citizenship. If foreigners become legal immigrants, resident aliens, or naturalized citizens, they are able to access some of the freedoms American citizens have. For decades legal immigrants and resident aliens seeking U.S. citizenship have renounced their allegiance to their former country and have served in the U.S. military all in an effort to acquire U.S. citizenship.

There are some privileges new legal immigrants, resident aliens, and naturalized citizens do not receive. They will be hard pressed to get a security clearance or work in federal security agencies where U.S. citizenship is a requirement. The Federal Aviation Administration and the Transportation Security Administration require U.S. citizenship and a ten-year background check. And they cannot become President of the United States. The requirement for that office is in Article II of the U.S. Constitution: “No person except a natural born citizen ... shall be eligible to the Office of President.”

Some foreigners who are on tourist or student visas seek to marry an American (for whatever timeframe the State Department required) to be able to apply for U.S. citizenship. Once the foreigner is able to trade his foreign passport for an American one, oftentimes the couple divorce and go their separate ways. For government immigration, naturalization, and citizenship professionals, this is the nature of the business.

For example, a topic that was rarely reported on by the media was the union of Barack Obama and Stanley Ann Dunham. Was this a union of two people in love? People with security clearances and jobs with the Immigration & Naturalization Service could have seen the marriage of Barack Obama, Senior and Stanley Ann Dunham as an obvious case of a legal contrivance, a marriage of convenience. In 1960-1, this was considered criminal activity and sixty years later, a marriage of convenience is still against the law.

There are thousands of couples every year who fall into the category of a suspected legal contrivance, a marriage of convenience. Couples may sometimes get together for reasons other than love: for political reasons, for monetary reasons, or for other personal reasons. But generally, marriage to an American is the quickest pathway for an alien or a foreigner to acquire U.S. citizenship. Sometimes children are produced to buttress a weak case. For Barack Obama’s mother, Stanley Ann Dunham, it may have been a case of a couple in love, or it may have been a case of a foreigner seeking the quickest pathway to U.S. citizenship. If it was a case of the latter, she may not have known she was being used. We do not have access to the investigator’s notes, so we will never know fully the details, but we do know the result of failure, Barack Obama, Senior was denied a green card and was deported in July 1964.

Over the course of their marriage, the actions of Barack Obama, Senior and Stanley Ann Dunham strongly suggest the I&NS denied any application for U.S. citizenship for the Kenyan national. The couple's response (divorce) could have been considered a classic case of a failed attempt of a marriage of convenience. But Immigration & Naturalization Service records relating to Barack Obama, Senior and Stanley Ann Dunham were sealed by court order after President Obama took office.

Many people in America see the example case of Barack Obama, Senior, like virtually all foreign students who come to America, as one person needing help with school and housing and food in order to escape the conditions in which they were once living. But not all foreigners come to America with honorable intentions. Some have ulterior motives.

For example, we were aware of companies that provided pilot training for foreign students. Those contracts (2007-10, post-9/11) centered on providing 12-14 Afghanistan air force officers with pilot training in Texas. One company that bid on the contract understood the dynamics and the flight risk of immature, unvetted, and unescorted foreign officers from an Islamic nation being in America. They suggested the Afghan officers receive approved flight training in another Muslim country where Islamic cultural sensitivities remain constant and there would be no flight risk; Muslim officers are rarely granted asylum in another Muslim country. That suggestion was ignored and the contract was awarded to another bidder. On three successive contract awards, 12-14 Afghanistan air force officers scheduled for pilot training in Texas disappeared within a week of their arrival. They left Texas for Canada where they sought and were granted asylum. Asylum was always the goal. These types of failures rarely reach the desk of a newspaper editor or a network producer. The FBI, the State Department, and others are notified, but what more can be done when Afghanistan air force officers seek asylum? Counterterrorism experts know through experience that there are some countries where conditions are so poor that people will do anything to escape.

But there is another side, a more evil side of the equation of foreign officers receiving pilot training in the United States. In early 2001, nearly two dozen men on foreign passports and tourist visas entered the United States. Some of them paid for flying lessons to learn how to fly a jet but not how to land it. Few warnings were raised; the FBI was informed but lost the trail of the bad guys. Then September 11, 2001 occurred and America changed. Americans are not used to dealing with international criminals and terrorists in disguise, *juramentados* in business suits or business casual who were hell-bent on killing Americans.

Professional counterterrorism people with some of the top security clearances study international criminals and mass murderers in the counterterrorism field. They work to protect American citizens and the homeland, not from Africans or Afghanis who seek citizenship or political asylum, but from the men who seek to kill Americans by the hundreds and thousands. These counterterrorism professionals receive specialized training and many are assigned overseas in locations where these terrorists live, train, and work. These people find that the world is a much more complicated and vicious place than anyone at the Mall of America could ever imagine. The backgrounds of these professionals are checked and rechecked; they voluntarily submit to polygraphs, all for the privilege of working in the intelligence community to protect Americans. These people have nothing to hide. People of the intelligence community welcome the polygraph; noteworthy, Democrats do not.

The backgrounds and lives of countless men and women of the intelligence community are open books, especially to investigators with clearances. Domestic and international criminals and jihadists go to the opposite extreme. They conduct their business in secret. They hide in the shadows. They do everything in their power to erase their backgrounds, hide their actions, activities, and associates. They try to conceal their identities.

Most Americans have very little idea of what the intelligence community actually does. Members of the intelligence community are at war with people committed to doing harm to America and Americans. The worst of those at war with America are the spies who seek to infiltrate the intelligence community. This was one of many goals of the former Union of Soviet Socialist Republics and the KGB, the *Komitet Gosudarstvennoy Bezopasnosti*; the foreign intelligence and domestic security agency of the Soviet Union.

An FBI Special Agent, W. Cleon Skousen, wrote *The Naked Communist* in 1958. He toured America to spread the message of his book, that the USSR determined they could not defeat us militarily or violently overthrow our government. But they could undermine America from within by planting spies to steal secrets for Moscow. Sometimes counterintelligence specialists found these spies through the polygraph. Sometimes the spies realized they had been fooled by the ideology and gave themselves up. They also identified the spies they had been working with or assisting, for example, Whittaker Chambers and Alger Hiss. Noteworthy, the left and the media rarely acknowledge how the *former* communist Chambers exposed the communist Alger Hiss as the greatest spy to have reached the top level in the U.S. government or how they used propaganda to try to discredit Chambers and the FBI while lionizing the urbane Hiss as a victim unduly charged. It's worth a few seconds to review the caliber of such a spy as Alger Hiss.

In 1944, Hiss was named Director of the Office of Special Political Affairs at the U.S. State Department. In February 1945, as a member of the U.S. delegation, Hiss attended the Yalta Conference where the Big Three, Franklin D. Roosevelt, Joseph Stalin, and Winston Churchill, met to consolidate and reaffirm their alliance. Hiss also participated in the meetings where the American draft of the "Declaration of Liberated Europe" was created. Here is a picture of Alger Hiss with Stalin, Roosevelt, and Churchill at Yalta:

Attendees at the Yalta Conference, February 4-11, 1945, Alger Hiss circled

On August 3, 1948, Whittaker Chambers[2], a former U.S. Communist Party member, testified under subpoena before the House Un-American Activities Committee (HUAC) that Hiss had secretly been a communist while in federal service. After a thorough review revealed just how thoroughly the U.S. intelligence community had been penetrated by the Soviet Union and the U.S. Communist Party, the polygraph machine was introduced and was utilized to weed out the potential infiltrators from the patriots.

Law enforcement may use a polygraph as a tool to interrogate a criminal suspect. Some federal government agencies, such as the organizations within the intelligence community, use polygraph examinations extensively for employees, contractors, and employee candidates. They rely on the American Polygraph Association to offer professional resources for evidence-based detection of deception through the use of polygraph.

The media, the Democrat Party, and their friendly attorneys hate the polygraph and are motivated to create an illusion that polygraph machines "are highly inaccurate, may easily be defeated by countermeasures, and are an imperfect or invalid means[3] of assessing truthfulness." Why is it that the leftist media and Democrats run away from taking polygraphs while those in the business of counter-intelligence, counter-espionage, and counter-terrorism welcome the electronic scrutiny as a necessary tool against infiltration? The system is not perfect but it has proven to be very effective. There is a group of people within our government who receive the highest level of classified information but are not required to take a polygraph: our politicians.

From the Revolutionary War there was no way to keep secrets from being stolen and used against the Continental Army and the Founding Fathers, other than drafting strict legislation to keep foreigners out of the government. The Founders felt it was especially important to prevent foreigners from entering the office of the ultimate decision maker, the President of the United States.

It is difficult to look at the domestic interpretation or autopsy of the election of 2008, 2012, 2016, or 2020 with all of the distractions and the lies of the media, the DNC, and Hollywood. Americans were obviously and maliciously being lied to non-stop. They were being manipulated in all of *dark psychology's* forms: propaganda, gaslighting, manipulation, lying by omission, behavior modification, insinuation, etc. Why? All so an ineligible candidate could win the election for the highest position in the land for four years?

Anyone who thinks the media is honest, accurate, and dedicated to providing factual information to Americans might want to consider this. While the U.S. military may have correspondents and journalists *embedded* with active duty troops from time to time, the men and women with top secret clearances in special operations forces, law enforcement, and the intelligence community are virtually prohibited from having any close contact with the media. The IC may contract for journalistic and media services; that is different from having a reporter, who has not been vetted and does not have a top secret clearance, have access to the work spaces of the men and women of the IC. Official government contact with the media is done through public affairs offices. Violations of these laws—euphemistically called leaks by the media—occur when government officials steal or turn over classified information to persons not authorized to see or possess it.

The most famous leaker was former FBI Deputy Director William Mark Felt, Sr., "*Deep Throat.*" He was described by the media as the anonymous government source who had leaked classified information to *Washington Post* reporters, Carl Bernstein and Bob Woodward. Felt, a Democrat, should have been prosecuted for espionage for passing classified information to the media who were not authorized to see or possess it. He only revealed his treason in hospice and took his treachery to his death.

There are multiple reasons for keeping the media away from classified information. When the media receives information, they generally want to report it. But another most insidious and detrimental reason is that sometimes the Fourth Estate functions as a Fifth Column. It cannot be trusted, for it functions no differently than the KGB of old. What this means is that the media does whatever is necessary, outside of official channels (like the KGB of old), to penetrate the intelligence community and gain access to the nation's most cherished secrets and special access programs, in order to use or publish the nation's secrets.

This provides fodder for further consideration. Former FBI Deputy Director Mark Felt leaked national secrets for ideological reasons. He hated President Nixon and prostituted himself and misused his office for personal gain in order to give the president's adversaries information possibly detrimental to the Presidential office. Let's not sugar coat it, Felt used the power of his office for personal reasons, he wanted to hurt the president, and in doing so violated his oath of office.

Felt violated his oath, functioned as a spy, and also identified domestic enemies; the people he gave the nation's secrets to, the media. Former FBI Deputy Director Felt used his office in the same manner as the former Director of the Office of Special Political Affairs, Alger Hiss, to cover his spying. Hiss gave Whittaker Chambers State Department secrets, while Felt gave the *Washington Post* reporters, Carl Bernstein and Bob Woodward the FBI's secrets. Those who leaned right politically, found Felt's and Hiss' actions treasonable. Those who leaned left politically (identified by their words and actions) found Felt's and Hiss' actions commendable.

Members of the military and the intelligence community have no problems identifying our foreign enemies. They have no issues with taking a polygraph. Identifying a domestic enemy can be more difficult. Consider Felt's and Hiss' actions. Felt used his position of "special trust and confidence" in the FBI to become a resource for the media. He would have (or should have) been prosecuted had his activities been discovered. There was evidence of Alger Hiss' treason, Chambers turned over copies of microfilm sent to the USSR that when printed out created a stack of documents 4 ½ feet tall, and Hiss went to jail.

So is it wrong to suspect some of the players of the 2008 election when counterintelligence professionals have seen the fingerprints of international criminals and terrorists doing what they can to infiltrate the U.S. government and gain access to America's secrets? Is it fair to look at and scrutinize a media that has become so corrupt that it actually engages in propaganda, disinformation, obfuscation, and abets international criminals and terrorists? For the moment, consider Al Jazeera which does that directly. The American media has only one or two degrees of separation from the Middle East posterchild of corrupt media, Al Jazeera.

Like spies working covertly in the intelligence community, there is a side of the media that is not on the side of America. The media works to dismantle America and hides behind the First Amendment to do it. They side with the left and use propaganda to lie to the American people while they aid and abet our enemies.

CHAPTER 15
THE EXPLANATORY MEMORANDUM AND A CURIOUS COINCIDENCE

In an earlier chapter, we referenced the working group formed by the Center for Security Policy called Team B II. It was made up of nearly two dozen very accomplished and experienced security professionals who published the findings of their analyses in SHARIAH: *The Threat to America*[1] from analyzing the contents of "An Explanatory Memorandum[2]," *From the Archives of the Muslim Brotherhood in America.*

In the introduction to the Explanatory Memorandum the author asked, "How do you like to see the Islam Movement in North America in ten years?" The answer is contained in a couple of interesting paragraphs which lists the general strategic goals of the Muslim Brotherhood in North America. These are:

1. Establishing an effective and stable Islamic Movement led by the Muslim Brotherhood.
2. Adopting Muslim's causes domestically and globally.
3. Expanding the observant Muslim base.
4. Unifying and directing Muslim efforts.
5. Presenting Islam as a civilization alternative.
6. Supporting the establishment of the global Islamic State wherever it is.

Now remember the words of the great Alexander Hamilton in The *Federalist Papers*: No. 68[3]: *Nothing was more to be desired than that every practicable obstacle should be opposed to cabal, intrigue, and corruption. These most deadly adversaries of republican government might naturally have been expected to make their approaches from more than one quarter, but chiefly from the desire in foreign powers to gain an improper ascendant in our councils. How could they better gratify this, than by raising a creature of their own to the chief magistracy of the Union?*

Has America fallen into the political impossibility "...of ambitious foreigners, who might otherwise be intriguing for the office actually penetrated the U.S. government and *the chief magistracy of the Union?*" Has America let her defenses down and allowed "...[the] *most deadly adversaries of republican government... to make their approaches from more than one quarter?*" Has America allowed "*...foreign powers to gain an improper ascendant in our councils?*" Would it be more accurate to say that one political party is dedicated to seeking power without regard to the law or oath of office, while the other political party works to stop their opponents?

Counterterrorism officials are loathe to admit but the evidence supports that in all probability we have witnessed the improper ascension of the son of a foreign national into the top job of the federal government. The media facilitated much of Barack Obama's success in winning the White House. If they hadn't used massive levels and diverse forms of propaganda, it might be a different story today. Many hundreds of people tried to stop him and the Democrat Party and to derail their radical agenda. There are things we can talk about today that we dared not fifteen years ago. Not only did people wonder how it all happened, they wondered, "Why?" We showed how it happened; we'd like a crack at answering, "Why?" There are many clues.

After several years researching the media's influence in the 2008 presidential election and the obvious ineligibility of one of the candidates, we became first concerned then alarmed at the level of energy the media expended to elect Barack Obama. It might not have been simply because the media hates Republicans and loves Democrats. The media long ago left their charter for fair and balanced reporting behind. We have seen something we had never seen before in our media—the active use and targeted application of Nazi-style propaganda.

The more we investigated the Democrats, Barack Obama, and the media, the more we found the fingerprints of evil. Did the media's malfeasance, disinformation, and censorship facilitate a "foreign power" to "*...rais[e] a creature of their own to the chief magistracy of the Union?*"

Let's look at one of those noteworthy documents, translated and now in the public domain, that illustrates the level of treachery encountered by counterterrorism experts. This is the preamble from the 2013 Center for Security Policy *An Explanatory Memorandum*: From the Archives of the Muslim Brotherhood in America[4]:

"We at the Center for Security Policy feel it is important for Americans to better understand—and, then, be able to successfully contend with—those that attempt to destroy or subvert our way of life. As making our nation's enemies' threat doctrines available is a key part of our educational efforts, we are pleased to present the blueprint for the Muslim Brotherhood in America, known as *An Explanatory Memorandum: On the General Strategic Goal for the Group in North America* or, in America's largest terrorist prosecution in US federal court, Government Exhibit 003-0085 3:04-CR-240-G in *U.S. v Holy Land Foundation, et al.*"

"In August of 2004, an alert Maryland Transportation Authority Police officer observed a woman wearing traditional Islamic garb videotaping the support structures of the Chesapeake Bay Bridge, and conducted a traffic stop. The driver was Ismail Elbarasse and he was detained on an outstanding material witness warrant issued in Chicago in connection with fundraising for Hamas. The FBI's Washington Field Office subsequently executed a search warrant on Elbarasse's residence in Annandale, Virginia. In the basement of his home, a hidden sub-basement was found; it revealed over 80 banker boxes of the archives of the Muslim Brotherhood in North America. One of the most important of these documents made public to date was entered into evidence during the Holy Land Foundation trial. It amounted to the Muslim Brotherhood's strategic plan for the United States and was entitled, '*An Explanatory Memorandum*: On the General Strategic Goal for the Group in North America.' The *Explanatory Memorandum* was written in 1991 by a member of the Board of Directors for the Muslim Brotherhood in North America and senior Hamas leader named Mohammed Akram. It had been approved by the Brotherhood's *Shura* Council and Organizational Conference and was meant for internal review by the Brothers' leadership in Egypt. It was certainly not intended for public consumption, particularly in the targeted society: the United States. For these reasons, the memo constitutes a Rosetta stone for the Muslim Brotherhood, its goals, modus operandi and infrastructure in America. It is arguably the single most important vehicle for understanding a secretive organization and should, therefore, be considered required reading for policy-makers and the public, alike."

"Another extraordinarily important element of the *Memorandum* is its attachment. Under the heading, 'A List of Our Organizations and Organizations of Our Friends,' Akram helpfully identified 29 groups as Muslim Brotherhood fronts. Many of them are even now, some twenty-two years later, still among the most prominent Muslim-American organizations in the United States. Worryingly, the senior representatives of these groups are routinely identified by U.S. officials as 'leaders' of the Muslim community in this country, to be treated as 'partners' in 'countering violent extremism' and other outreach initiatives. Obviously, this list suggests such treatment translates into vehicles for deep penetration of the American government and civil society."

Key findings from the study include the following:

"The United States is under attack by foes who are openly animated by what is known in Islam as *shariah* (Islamic law). According to *shariah*, every faithful Muslim is obligated to wage *jihad*, whether violent or not, against those who do not adhere to this comprehensive, totalitarian, political-military code. The enemy's explicit goal is to establish a global Islamic State, known as the caliphate, governed by *shariah*."

"*Shariah* is based on the Quran (held by all Muslims to be the 'uncreated' word of Allah as dictated to Mohammed), *hadiths* (sayings of Mohammed), and agreed interpretations. It commands Muslims to carry out *jihad* (holy war) indefinitely until all of the *Dar al-Harb* (i.e., the House of War, where *shariah* is not enforced) is brought under the domination of *Dar al-Islam* (the House of Islam–or literally the House of Submission, where *shariah is* enforced)."

"*Shariah* dictates that non-Muslims be given three choices: convert to Islam and conform to *shariah*; submit as second-class citizens (*dhimmis*); or be killed. Not all classes are given the second option."

"Both Islamic terrorism and pre-violent, 'civilization *jihad*' (popularly referred to as 'stealth jihad') are commanded by *shariah*. That is not only the view of 'extremists' and 'fringe' elements 'hijacking the religion,' but of many authorities of Islam widely recognized as mainstream and drawing upon orthodox texts, interpretations and practices of the faith."

"The Muslim Brotherhood is the font of modern Islamic *jihad.* It is dedicated to the same global supremacist objectives as those (like al-Qaeda and the Taliban) who share its adherence to *shariah* but who believe that violent *jihad* is more likely to more quickly produce the common goal of a global caliphate."

"The Brotherhood's internal documents make clear that civilization *jihad* is subversion waged by stealth instead of violence only until such time as Muslims are powerful enough to progress to violent *jihad* for the final conquest."

"Those who work to insinuate *shariah* into the United States intend to subvert and replace the Constitution (itself a violation of Article VI) because, according to *shariah*, freedom of religion, other civil liberties enshrined in the Constitution, and the rule of man-made law are incompatible with *Islam* (which means 'submission')."

"The *shariah*-adherent enemy prioritizes information warfare, manifested in American society as propaganda, political warfare, psychological warfare, influence operations and subversion of our foundational institutions. Our government structure fails to recognize this strategy because it is focused so exclusively on kinetic attacks. As a result, the United States remains crippled in its inability to engage this enemy effectively on his primary battlefield."

"The Brotherhood exploits the atmosphere of intimidation created by Islamic terrorists, thus inculcating in the West a perceived need for 'outreach' to the 'Muslim community' which, in turn, opens up opportunities to pursue a campaign of stealthy infiltration into American and other Western societies. The combined effect of such 'civilization *jihad*' and *jihadism* of the violent kind may prove to be considerably more dangerous for this country and other Western societies than violent *jihad* alone."

"The Brotherhood has succeeded in penetrating our educational, legal and political systems, as well as top levels of government, intelligence, the media, and U.S. military, virtually paralyzing our ability to plan or respond effectively."

"Muslim Brotherhood organizations conduct outreach to the government, law enforcement, media, religious community, and others for one reason: to subvert them in furtherance of their objective, which is implementation of Islamic law."

"An informed and determined counter-strategy to defend the Constitution from *shariah* can yet succeed—provided it is undertaken in the prompt, timely and comprehensive manner recommended by Team B II."

We keyed on the following—italicized for emphasis: "The Brotherhood's internal documents make clear that '*...civilization jihad is subversion waged by stealth instead of violence*' only until such time as Muslims are powerful enough to progress to violent *jihad* for the final conquest."

When the Muslim Brotherhood documents advocate "stealth instead of violence," is this a direct reference to one of the silent weapons of the quiet war on America; was the Muslim Brotherhood also engaged in *propaganda*?

RationalWiki[5] was quick to offer: "There is no evidence that a plot to actually accomplish this exists, that this is one of the Muslim Brotherhood's goals, or that the Memorandum was even seen by anyone besides its author until it was discovered during the investigation. The writing style of the Arabic original was also deemed peculiar after linguistic analysis, and many of the neologisms in the Memorandum, such as 'civilizational *jihad*,' show no evidence of spreading."

Is that true? Is that propaganda? Is there anyone out there connecting the dots? It seems there might be at least one person.

We now present a November 3, 2016 *American Thinker*[6] article (used with permission) where the author notes, somewhat tongue-in-cheek, but with obvious deadly earnest: "In the 2000s, one of America's legends is the pioneer community organizer, Barack Obama, aka Barry Shariaseed. Barry Shariaseed wanders the Christian communities of the world planting the seeds of Islam in an effort to introduce Muslims into the Christian world. No one ever questioned his Muslim faith[7] as he extended the *shariah* wherever he traveled. Over the years, his frequent visits to government agencies were looked forward to, and no United Nations door was ever closed to him. To the men of the Muslim Brotherhood he was 'The One' they've been waiting for.[8] He was also very religious and mandated the *shariah* to people along the way. His favorite sound was the Call to Prayer[9]. (Apologies to the story of Johnny Appleseed[10].)

"A recent WikiLeaks release of a 'Podesta email' reminded us of a document submitted into evidence during America's largest terrorist prosecution in U.S. federal court, *U.S. v. Holy Land Foundation, et al.* The Center for Security Policy posted the Muslim Brotherhood's Strategic Plan in America. This document is known in counterterrorism circles as *An Explanatory Memorandum: On the General Strategic Goal for the Group in North America.* The Center for Security Policy also published the 2010 *SHARIAH*: The Threat to America: An Exercise in Competitive Analysis. Some of the authors of the analysis are well known inside and outside the intelligence community, such as Lt. Gen. William Jerry Boykin."

"The innocuous-sounding Explanatory Memorandum explained how the Muslim Brotherhood sought to extend *shariah* into the United States and Canada. The document outlined the mission of the Muslim Brother in North America through a five-phase plan[11]. Specifically, [t]he process of settlement is a 'Civilization-Jihadist Process.' The *Ikhwan* must understand that their work in America is a kind of grand *jihad* in eliminating and destroying the Western civilization from within and 'sabotaging' its miserable house by their hands and the hands of the believers so that it is eliminated and God's religion is made victorious over all other religions."

"*Ikhwan* refers to the local or stealthy jihadis of North America and not the Wahhabi religious militia made up of nomadic tribesmen in Saudi Arabia."

"Under *shariah*, civilization *jihad*[12]—a 'pre-violent' form of *jihad*—is considered an integral, even dominant element of *jihad* that is at least as obligatory for *shariah's* adherents as the violent kind. Such tactics are ostensibly 'nonviolent'—not because the Muslim Brotherhood eschews violence, but because the Explanatory Memorandum has decided that this strategic phase of battlefield preparation is better accomplished through stealthy means. Hence, civilization *jihad* can be considered 'stealth *jihad*.'"

"The Ikhwan's strategy for destroying the United States[13] is to get us, specifically our leadership, to do the bidding of the Muslim Brotherhood for them. The Muslim Brotherhood intends to conduct Civilization *Jihad* by co-opting our leadership *into believing a counterfactual understanding of*

Islam and the nature of the Muslim Brotherhood, thereby coercing these leaders to enforce the Muslim Brotherhood narrative on their subordinates."

"Another document referenced from the *U.S. v. Holy Land Foundation* trial was an undated paper entitled '*Phases of the World Underground Movement Plan*[14].' It specified the five phases of the Muslim Brotherhood Movement in North America. They are described, together with comments about the *Ikhwan's* progress in realizing each goal." Here are two "phases."

Phase One: Phase of discreet and secret establishment of leadership.

Phase Two: Phase of gradual appearance on the public scene and exercising and utilizing various public activities. Establishing a shadow government (secret) within the Government.

"The memory-triggering Podesta email[15] came from former New York solicitor general Preeta D. Bansal, sent to a classmate of then-candidate Obama and a member of the Obama campaign's transition team. What caught our eye was this (emphasis added): '*In the candidates for top jobs*, I excluded those with some Arab American background but who are not Muslim (e.g., George Mitchell). Many Lebanese Americans, for example, are Christian. In the last list (of outside boards/commissions), most who are listed appear to be Muslim American, except that a handful (where noted) may be Arab American but of uncertain religion (esp. Christian).' A generous review of the email assessed that the 2007 Obama transition team clearly had planned to hire Muslims over Christians *for the top jobs* and gave early preferential treatment to Muslims over everyone else."

"While the Podesta email may look like 'not much' at face value, the emphasis on adherence to the *Phases of the World Underground Movement Plan* is significant, given other troubling aspects of the Obama administration. A disturbing pattern of implementing Phase One and Two activities emerged after the election of President Obama."

"President Obama told NASA Administrator Charles Bolden that his highest priority should be '...to find a way to reach out to the Muslim world[16] and engage much more with dominantly Muslim nations to help them feel good about their historic contribution to science...and math and engineering.' NASA went on a Muslim hiring spree, as did other government agencies."

"With the election of President Obama in November 2008 and his Muslim Outreach initiative, exemplified by his Cairo 'A New Beginnings[17]' speech at Al Azhar University, the Obama administration extended a formal welcome to the Muslim Brotherhood. *Investor's Business Daily*[18] noted a lengthy chronology of events in support of the Muslim Brotherhood, punctuated by the overthrow of the Mubarak regime in Egypt during the Arab Spring of 2011 that swept the Muslim Brotherhood into power. In 2009, the White House invited the Islamic Society of North America (ISNA) president to President Obama's inauguration ceremonies, even though the Justice Department just two years earlier had blacklisted the Brotherhood affiliate as an unindicted co-conspirator in the Holy Land trial. Obama delivered his Cairo speech, infuriating the Mubarak regime by inviting Muslim Brotherhood leaders to attend. In 2011, the Brotherhood vowed to tear up Egypt's 30-year peace treaty with Israel. Since Mubarak's fall, the Muslim Brotherhood has worked to re-establish Cairo's ties with Hamas and Hezb'allah."

"Sensitive and top-level government positions have been filled by Muslims with questionable loyalties to the United States. One of the FBI's former top experts on Islam announced that President Obama's pick to head the Central Intelligence Agency, John Brennan, converted to Islam years ago[19]. Hillary Clinton's top campaign aide, Huma Abedin, edited a radical Muslim publication[20] that blamed the U.S. for 9/11. Syed Abedin[21], the father of Huma, outlined his Muslim Brotherhood view of *shariah* law and how the Western world has turned Muslims 'hostile.'"

"Closely associated with *shariah* doctrine on lying is the concept of *taqiya*[22], which is generally described as lying for the sake of Islam. *Taqiya* permits and encourages precautionary dissimulation as a means for hiding true faith in times of persecution or deception when penetrating the enemy camp."

"The enemy camp is the United States of America, and we are the targets of a stealthy *jihad*. The Muslim Brotherhood's Strategic Plan is being implemented. Led by Barry Shariaseed, aka Barack Obama, who has planted the seeds of *shariah* wherever he goes, the Muslim Brotherhood has infiltrated the U.S. at the highest levels of government. Infiltration will be total with the election of Hillary Clinton and her Muslim Brotherhood proxy, Huma Abedin."

These heavily referenced articles put new emphasis on the findings of SHARIAH: *The Threat to America* and "An Explanatory Memorandum," *From the Archives of the Muslim Brotherhood in America* and the election of President Obama and his Administration. The aforementioned articles demonstrate that the Obama Administration was actively engaged in a stealthy *jihad*, domestically and internationally and that the White House and the State Department were central to facilitating Muslim Brotherhood activities. They established or furthered the Islamic Movement led by the Muslim Brotherhood across Africa. They adopted Muslim causes domestically and globally, from "hiring Muslims for the top jobs" to "Muslim outreach programs" in the Muslim world led by NASA and other U.S. institutions, cabinet positions, departments and agencies. The Obama Administration expanded the observant Muslim base and unified and directed Muslim efforts, forcing major government institutions such as the FBI and the DOD to engage in Muslim outreach. The president presented Islam as a civilization alternative and supported the establishment of the global Islamic State wherever it was, orchestrating the fall of U.S. allies in the Muslim world—Egypt, Algeria, Tunisia, Libya—and fostering the replacement governments with U.S.-backed Muslim Brotherhood candidates as heads of state.

Was this stealthy *jihad*? Was the Muslim Brotherhood or any Islamic group actually making inroads into the U.S. government? Suppression by U.S. media outlets have made it virtually impossible to report evidence of this in the United States. Some people in the Obama campaign accused Republicans of pushing multiple conspiracy theories about Obama's religion and supposed ties to Islam. They repeated ad nauseum, as if it were a chant, "There's no evidence." Then in a January 2018 article run by the British *Daily Mail*[23], a journalist revealed a 13-year-old photo of Barack Obama posing with the Nation of Islam's leader, Louis Farrakhan. This photo had been kept secret "in order to protect President Obama's career."

The Daily Mail detailed how Askia Muhammad snapped the photo of Obama smiling alongside the Reverend Louis Farrakhan during a Congressional Black Caucus (CBC) meeting in 2005. Askia Muhammad, who revealed the photo, said that he gave the picture up at the time and basically swore secrecy out of concern that it could have damaged Obama's political future.

Why would it damage Barack Hussein Obama's future to be seen smiling with men from the Nation of Islam?

Muhammad told the news site that the photo was kept a secret until after Obama secured the Democratic nomination to run for president, "all the way up until the inauguration." It was kept under cover for the eight years Obama was president.

He recalled that a staff member for the CBC "sort of in a panic" called him after he took the photo. "I sort of understood what was going on," Muhammad said. He made arrangements to give the picture to Leonard Farrakhan, the minister's son-in-law and chief of staff. He said he gave away "the disk" from his camera but "copied the photograph from that day onto a [computer] file." "Realizing that I had given it up, I mean, it was sort of like a promise to keep the photograph secret," Muhammad said.

Quoting from the Religio-Political Talk[24] (RPT) website on the topic of the Reverend Wright's Trinity United Church of Christ's AKIBA Bookstore, were several comments made by Harvard Professor Emeritus, Alan Dershowitz that suggest Senator Obama's relationships with Louis Farrakhan was a disqualifier for public office. He said, "That any Democrat who meets with the 'bigot' Louis Farrakhan should resign from office." Professor Dershowitz insisted that "...there should be no tolerance for any association with the Nation of Islam."

"Farrakhan is a bigot," Dershowitz said on Fox News. "He is far worse than David Duke. Why? Because Farrakhan has a large following, David Duke is a joke."

Professor Dershowitz continued, "He ought to be treated the way we treat David Duke," he said. "If any Republican dared to meet with David Duke, that would be the end of their career. It should be the end of the career of any Democrat who has any association with this bigot Farrakhan." Dershowitz added, "This is the leadership of the Democratic Party."

On February 5, 2014, in a *Washington Free Beacon*[25] article, a senior member of the Muslim Brotherhood was hosted at the White House for a meeting with President Barack Obama, prompting an outcry from critics of the global Islamist organization. Several quotes from the article are illuminating.

"Anas Altikriti, a top British lobbyist for the Muslim Brotherhood whose father heads Iraq's Muslim Brotherhood party, met with the President and Vice President Joe Biden as part of a delegation to discuss Iraq."

"Altikriti, whose work had also been tied to Hamas, is seen smiling in photos published by the White House as he stood next to Iraqi Parliament Speaker Usama al-Nujaifi, who is pictured shaking hands with President Obama in the White House's Roosevelt Room."

The meeting was not covered by the American news media and was first reported by the United Kingdom blog Harry's Place[26]. The Obama administration has been criticized for its outreach to the Muslim Brotherhood, the international Islamist organization whose members' brief reign in Egypt was supported by the White House.

"Altikriti's presence in the White House was surprising to many who said the U.K. organization he heads, the Cordoba Foundation, has been singled out by British Prime Minister David Cameron as the political front for the Muslim Brotherhood[27]." Paul Stott, an U.K. academic and expert in British jihadism at the University of East Anglia, said Altikriti's presence in the meetings represented, quote: "...part of the long-term U.S.-U.K. engagement with the Muslim Brotherhood, a strategy which hit choppy waters when it became clear people in Egypt were far from ready to let the Muslim Brotherhood run the country the way they wanted."

Quote: Altikriti has been called the key political lobbyist for the Muslim Brotherhood in Britain.

According to the *Washington Free Beacon* article, Nujaifi, Altikriti, and other members of the Iraqi delegation just happened to be in town late January to discuss al-Qaeda's growing presence in Iraq. Nujaifi was reported to have met with President Obama twice, though it was unclear if Altikriti accompanied him on both occasions.

The *Washington Free Beacon* provided the White House's photograph and caption showed President Obama greeting Speaker Osama al-Nujaifi, Iraqi Council of Representatives, in the Roosevelt Room of the White House with Altikriti standing to al-Nujaifi's right side.

So there were secret photographs of Candidate Obama with the Nation of Islam's leader, Louis Farrakhan. There were secret photographs of President Obama and Muslim leaders, and there were meetings in the White House with the leaders of the Muslim Brotherhood that were not covered by the U.S. media. The Obama Administration bent over backward to allow unfettered immigration of Muslims from African nations while pushing Muslim outreach initiatives in the U.S. government.

Without the context of the Muslim Brotherhood's *Explanatory Memorandum* (the strategic plan to infiltrate America), without the context of the *Phases of the World Underground Movement Plan,* "Phase of discreet and secret establishment of leadership," the "Phase of gradual appearance on the public scene and exercising and utilizing various public activities, and [e]stablishing a shadow government (secret) within the Government," the actions of the Obama White House to direct Muslim Outreach initiatives to senior officials may look a little like prerogatives of the office. The president was simply trying to right old wrongs in the Muslim world.

But that statement is also propaganda. A BIG LIE.

Taking the Muslim Brotherhood's *Explanatory Memorandum* and the *Phases of the World Underground Movement Plan* in context with the White House actions, a reasonable person can finally understand what was meant by, "Change will not come if we wait for some other person or some other time. We are the ones we've been waiting for. We are the change that we seek[28]."

He that walketh with wise men shall be wise: but a companion of fools shall be destroyed. (This well-known saying is a short and weak version of Solomon's true warning. *You are the company you keep.*)

–Proverbs 13:20

CHAPTER 16
WHEN DONALD TRUMP AND BARACK OBAMA'S PATHS CROSSED

Before Barack Obama oozed onto the national stage as the keynote speaker at the Democrat National Convention in 2004, Donald J. Trump was a Democrat billionaire with a television show, a jet and a helicopter, skyscraper hotels and golf courses, and an exotic model wife.

Before running for president, Barack Obama took credit for writing two autobiographies, even though he couldn't write an article as the president of the Harvard Law Review. Neither did he write the highly marketed *Journeys in Black and White.* He had an unremarkable career as a teacher and a lawyer, and as a Chicago politician. He also had some interesting, politically radical acquaintances. He admitted to being part of the dope-smoking, cocaine-using, Choom Gang. Barack Obama had a drug-fueled radical past that his Department of Justice and his campaign tried to cover up through court-ordered sealed records. He needed a job that didn't require urinalysis.

The Apprentice star, Donald J. Trump didn't touch alcohol. He was the polar opposite of Barack Hussein Obama.

Donald Trump was a friend of the Clintons and didn't believe Obama was eligible. So in 2008, Hillary Clinton secured The Donald's endorsement: "I know Hillary and I think she'd make a great president or vice-president." During her campaign, Candidate Clinton questioned the legitimacy of Barack Obama's citizenship through surrogate investigators. Barack Hussein Obama II was the child born in the unambiguous State of Hawaii to a Kenyan father and an American mother. Trump was annoyed that Senator Obama didn't drop out of the race. Obama was not a "natural born citizen."

Across the nation, professional, learned, and military men filed lawsuits to challenge the eligibility of Barack Obama to be president. The former Deputy Attorney General of Pennsylvania and a lifelong Democrat,

Philip J. Berg, filed a lawsuit[1] to force Barack Obama to produce a certified copy of his original birth certificate to prove that he could run for the office of President of the United States and could serve as the Commander in Chief. The DNC filed a motion[2] to dismiss the Berg action along with all the other lawsuits. The cause for dismissal always focused on standing. Only those who would be materially harmed in some way by the election of the candidate possessed standing. If Hillary Clinton had filed a lawsuit, she would have had standing. Berg and the others did not.

Questions remained. The American media jumped into high gear with disinformation campaigns and other psychological operations. McClatchy Washington Bureau Chief James Asher, the investigative editor in charge of Africa coverage, assigned a reporter to go to Kenya[3]. That reporter determined that the allegations of Barack Obama being born in Kenya were false. Investigators found archived newspapers in Hawaii that announced the birth of Barack Obama in Honolulu.

2008 Presidential candidate Alan Keyes testified that Barack Obama admitted to his Kenya birth in a debate with Keyes when running for U.S. Senate in Illinois in 2004. In a 2009 article[4], Dr. Jerome Corsi, a person of interest who ignominiously popped up during the Mueller investigation, asked, “Did Obama’s grandmother say he was born in Kenya?” When Dr. Corsi travelled to Kenya to ask the same questions as James Asher’s investigative reporter, he was nearly killed before being deported. Media coverage was relentless and stinging. Media mavens branded anyone questioning the eligibility of Barack Obama as the most reviled people on the planet, extremely toxic “birthers.”

This was very powerful and effective propaganda that spread across the country via the media. *Counter-propaganda* measures were less effective, portrayed as some dudes who were investigating the eligibility of the president. Investigators stayed away from any reference to birth certificates. Owners of blogs refused to run articles on any direct or implied questions of Obama’s eligibility.

Questions continued in large part because Republican leaders and right-leaning pundits and academics were not savvy enough to recognize propaganda for what it was and didn’t know how to combat it. They took a pass, refused to stand up and make their voices heard. The left’s over-the-top turbocharged propaganda operation on the birther issue made it radioactive virtually overnight, so no one in their right mind dared to investigate. The skillful application of hot-button words put all investigators on notice. *This area is off limits!* We were reminded of another subtle threat from SHARIAH: *The Threat to America*:

Shariah dictates that non-Muslims be given three choices: convert to Islam and conform to *shariah*; submit as second-class citizens (*dhimmis*); or be killed. Not all classes are given the second option.

In those early days there was a lot of chum being tossed in turbulent political waters as distractions. A standard campaign would have had a superlative credentialed candidate with a clean police record, distinguished military service, and a model family. All of those family members would know to stand and cover their hearts for the National Anthem. We saw just the opposite in the Obama campaign. Chaos seemed to surround Barack Obama. From the moment he stepped out onto the political stage he sought sympathy for the difficulties in his life. He came from a mixed-race home. He and his mother were rejected by his father. He was forced to attend the madrassas. He went to Columbia, but he was never accepted by his peers because of his mixed race. He was a victim of all these circumstances. Portraying oneself as a victim is a propaganda technique.

Consider this truly random reader's comment for *Dreams From My Father*: "In this lyrical, unsentimental, and compelling memoir, the son of a black African father and a white American mother searches for a workable meaning to his life as a black American. It begins in New York, where Barack Obama learns that his father—a figure he knows more as a myth than as a man—has been killed in a car accident. This sudden death inspires an emotional odyssey—first to a small town in Kansas, from which he retraces the migration of his mother's family to Hawaii, and then to Kenya, where he meets the African side of his family, confronts the bitter truth of his father's life, and at last reconciles his divided inheritance." He should have had a fairytale life as a black man instead of a life as a multiracial man who struggled with the rejection of his white peers. He is to be pitied. And that book was just part one.

This is raw propaganda and it was used masterfully. It is no different from Adolf Hitler's second autobiography[5], *Mein Kampf, My Struggle*.

Instead of blaming white men for a lousy life, Hitler blamed the Jewish people. He was the ultimate victim. But with *Mein Kampf, My Struggle*, the victim became the manipulator who used propaganda to hide and implement his plan, *The Final Solution*. Like Hitler, Obama's actions in office demonstrated an incredible animus toward white people. The President of the United States took the side of black men who were killed by white police officers and martyred them, before there was any investigation, and blaming law enforcement as racists. In his books, he expressed his animus of white people, so the victim became the manipulator who used propaganda to hide and implement his plan, *Muslim Outreach.*

In 2012, Donald Trump began pushing the issue of Obama's birth certificate in television interviews as he considered whether to run against President Obama. "I have some real doubts," Trump told the "Today" show[6]. He claimed to have sent his own investigators to Hawaii, where Obama was born. "I have people that actually have been studying it and they cannot believe what they're finding." Trump raised another issue in an interview with "Good Morning America," suggesting Obama was trying to conceal his religion by withholding his birth certificate. "Maybe it says he's a Muslim," he said.

Was Obama's religion ever an issue? Let's look at the religious affiliation of the last fifteen presidents:

POTUS	**Episcopalian**
32	Franklin D. Roosevelt
38	Gerald R. Ford
41	George H. W. Bush
	Presbyterian
34	Dwight D. Eisenhower
40	Ronald Reagan
45	Donald J. Trump
	Baptist
33	Harry S. Truman
39	Jimmy Carter
42	William J. Clinton
	Methodist
43	George W. Bush

	Disciples of Christ
36	Lyndon B. Johnson
	Roman Catholic
35	John F. Kennedy
	Quaker
31	Herbert Hoover
37	Richard M. Nixon
	Unaffiliated
44	Barack Hussein Obama

Nothing jumps out at us from this but we will look at the religion of Obama's father and its ramifications in a later chapter.

To the outrage of the women on the "The View[7]," Donald Trump sat on the sofa with Barbara Walters and Whoopi Goldberg and said, "There's something on that birth certificate that he doesn't like." Well before President Trump became a candidate, he offered millions of dollars for proof[8] that President Obama was born in the U.S. Trump said in 2014, "Pick your charity, for $50 million, and let me see your records! And I never heard from him." The media launched themselves into overdrive with thundering propaganda to counter Trump's statements. A few days before the 2012 presidential elections, businessman Donald Trump implored Barack Obama[9] to release *all of his records*, his college transcripts, and passport records[10] not just a birth certificate. When nothing was released from the White House, Donald Trump told Mother Jones magazine, "I am proud of the fact that I was able to get President Obama to release his birth certificate[11]."

Lawyers like Obama and Clinton should be familiar with the legal issue known as "spoliation of evidence." When parties fail to produce relevant evidence within their span of control, evidence which they are otherwise naturally expected to possess, the U.S. legal system allows and even mandates that unfavorable presumptions be drawn against them. When an item of relevant evidence—whether documents, physical objects, or data relevant to an ongoing legal matter—is destroyed, discarded or modified in any way, the U.S. legal system presumes that the missing evidence was unfavorable to that party and draws conclusions accordingly.

Spoliation of evidence is prohibited by an array of laws and regulations. Anyone who destroys relevant evidence or assists in such destruction is subject to criminal prosecution, civil fines, tort liability, exclusion of testimony and dismissal of claims, as well as adverse evidentiary inferences. Intentional destruction or negligent loss of evidence suggests that the party in possession believed that it was harmful to them, and that consciousness of guilt led them to destroy, hide or lose it.

Nothing screams "spoliation of evidence" and being over the target like having records sealed from the prying eyes of the Republican Party and Donald Trump and his millions. Intentionally sealing those records suggested that Obama believed exposing them would be harmful to him. If they were ever to be released, it is reasonable to expect that Obama would be exposed as a fraud. But what kind of fraud? The Democrats' worst nightmare would occur. America's first black president would be utterly destroyed and his accomplishments delegitimized. Exposure would also demonstrate the Democrat Party-media complex corruption was absolute and that the Muslim Brotherhood's infiltration was greater than anyone would have ever guessed.

Who were the lawyers who sealed all of President Obama's records? Dr. Orly Taitz posted on her website[12] that President Obama "has paid more than $5 million in legal fees[13] to national law firm Perkins Coie to keep his personal, and possibly professional, records hidden from the public." Obama appointed a partner at Perkins Coie, Robert Bauer, as White House Counsel ten months after taking office in 2009. Bauer also served as general counsel for the Democratic National Committee and "Obama for America" presidential campaign.

Americans have recently come to know that the law firm Perkins Coie had been retained by the Clinton campaign and the Democratic National Committee "to conduct research into allegations about Donald Trump's connections with Russians and possible coordination between his campaign and the Kremlin[14]." Marc E. Elias was a Perkins Coie lawyer representing the Clinton campaign and the DNC-retained Fusion GPS. Fusion GPS hired dossier author Christopher Steele, a former British intelligence officer with ties to the FBI and the American intelligence community.

So, the law firm entrusted to seal all of President Obama's records from Donald Trump and the American people was the same law firm at the center of the conspiracy to frame Donald Trump for Russian collusion and obstruction. The redacted Mueller report found no collusion or obstruction.

President Donald Trump wasn't just a burr under the saddle of Barack Obama. Donald Trump was a national personality who fearlessly and openly questioned the legitimacy of President Obama. Hollywood and the media cut ties with Donald Trump and attempted to paint him as a racist, but those efforts largely failed. Mr. Trump had billions of dollars, he had many African American friends of stature, and he could not be intimidated by either the media or the Democrats. They couldn't threaten him with the loss of his job or with never-ending lawsuits. "The Donald" could buy the best legal advice; he was impervious to ridicule, and he was persistent. He would not be dissuaded, knowing the flak is greatest when you are over the target. When the left engaged in increasingly vicious forms of propaganda, they were in essence announcing not only was he over the target, but that he was correct.

No matter what obstacle or distraction they threw in his way, from unrelenting shouts of racism to birtherism to Islamophobia, the media and the Democrats could not stop Donald Trump's pursuit of the truth they had so cleverly hidden from the American public. It was obvious the Democrat Party and the media were protecting President Obama.

Obama's hatred for Trump grew with every year of his presidency. If Obama was going to exact revenge on Trump, he would have to destroy the man in the eyes of his wife, his children, and his family. Trump claimed he had been audited "for 12 years, or something like that." In other words, he was audited by the IRS every year[15] of the Obama presidency. Twelve years of IRS audits didn't deter Trump. The ultimate revenge fantasy for President Obama, the Democrats, and the media would have been for Trump to be handcuffed and frog-marched out of the Trump Tower or later, the White House.

President Obama was the ultimate decision maker in the use of the full force of the U.S. government to kill candidate and then President Trump, not by bullet or bomb, but by propaganda, proxy, and paper—stunningly, egregiously embarrassing and felonious propaganda (Russian collusion) and paper (the Steele *dossier*).

International intelligence communities have incredible capabilities to manufacture counterfeit documents, establish credible false histories, and leverage their relationships with the media to place bogus stories into newspapers. Nixon needed help in finding out what the DNC was doing; Obama needed help in exacting revenge. Who had the specific skillset for such an endeavor? The Communist Party USA-voting CIA Director, John Brennan[16]. After he left office, did Barack Obama use everything in his power to destroy Donald Trump? Was it because President Trump knew President Obama should never have been elected since he was not eligible? Or was it because Trump outed Obama's clandestine Muslims in the government, stopped the unrestricted flow into America of undocumented Muslims from some of the world's worst hellholes, and cancelled all of his Muslim outreach initiatives?

Maybe it was both.

CHAPTER 17
IT'S HAPPENING AGAIN WITH KAMALA HARRIS

A recent Twitter exchange perfectly illustrates the laziness of the media, as well as their incompetence and arrogance on a topic they know nothing about. Instead of conducting a little research, which they could do with their smartphones, they pluck some nebulous and unnamed authority from the ether and cite that person's expertise as the gospel. A classic example occurred on July 12, 2019, the deputy director of rapid response for Media Matters for America[1] attacked Fox News' Tucker Carlson on what the "AR" in AR-15 stood for.

Andrew Lawrence @ndrew_lawrence
Tucker Carlson doesn't seem to understand that the "AR" in AR-15 stands for "Assault Rifle"
6,661
7:35 PM - Jul 12, 2019

Jacob Perry @RealJacobPerry
Replying to @ndrew_lawrence
That's because it doesn't
2,600
7:41 PM - Jul 12, 2019

Andrew Lawrence @ndrew_lawrence
Replying to @RealJacobPerry yes it does
717
7:41 PM - Jul 12, 2019

Andrew Lawrence @ndrew_lawrence

Replying to @ndrew_lawrence @RealJacobPerry just spoke with a troop who confirmed that indeed, the "AR" stands for "Assault Rifle"

1,190

7:42 PM - Jul 12, 2019

Helot @Helot_

Replying to @ndrew_lawrence @RealJacobPerry

This only confirms that not only you are an idiot, but the people you know are idiots also. AR in AR-15 stands for ARmalite. The AR-5 for instance was a bolt action rifle.

https://en.wikipedia.org/wiki/ArmaLite_AR-5...

1,169

8:10 PM - Jul 12, 2019

Andrew Lawrence @ndrew_lawrence

Replying to @Helot_ @RealJacobPerry nope im sorry it stands for "Assault Rifle" I just spoke with a troop who confirmed this to me. furthermore the 15 stands for the 15th gun invented (also confirmed by a troop) so the AR-5 was the 5th gun invented. check your facts

161

8:11 PM - Jul 12, 2019

Oemy @oemtechMMF

Replying to @ndrew_lawrence and 2 others

The AR stands for Armalite Rifle model 15. It was designed by Eugene Stoner as a lighter version of the AR-10. Armalie sold the AR10 & AR15 to Colt. Colt did some redesign and sold the rifle to the US Government as the M16.

40

5:23 PM - Jul 13, 2019

Recently, the issue of natural born citizenship of a presidential candidate came up again and the media again citied presumably credible sources.

Under the heading of, *Yes, Kamala Harris is eligible to run for President*[2], the author, Louis Jacobson, cites a familiar refrain from Barack Obama's run for president: "So the key language is whether Harris is a 'natural born citizen.' And experts say she meets that definition."

Like the "troop" who presumably had expert knowledge that the AR in AR-15 meant assault rifle, Mr. Jacobson, a Politifact contributor, rolled out his cherry-picked ignorant-of-the-subject-matter experts who cited:

"If you are born in the U.S, you are automatically a natural-born U.S. citizen under the constitution," said Harvard Law Professor Einer Elhauge. And two other law professors with presumed expertise in this area—Mary Brigid McManamon of Widener University and Malinda L. Seymore of Texas A&M University—agreed that Harris is clearly eligible.

Sarah Duggin, a Catholic University law professor, also agrees. "Her birth in the United States, to someone other than a member of a foreign diplomatic corps or otherwise not subject to U.S. jurisdiction, makes her a U.S. citizen unless she later renounced her citizenship. There is no reason to look at where her parents came from, how long her parents were U.S. residents before she was born, or where she was raised." *There is no reason to look at where her parents came from?* Sarah Duggin is quite mad and/or a pathetic ideologue. She must have missed that whole lesson on citizenship at law school—maybe in its place they are now teaching critical race theory or Marxism 101.

Capitalizing on the residual propaganda left over from the Obama years, the media tried to leverage unadulterated lies as the gospel, another Illusion of Truth. Goebbels would be stunned at the leftist media's arrogance and turpitude, if he wasn't turning on a rotisserie in Hell, he'd be standing and applauding.

There was no point in seeking to convert the intellectuals. For intellectuals would never be converted and would anyway always yield to the stronger, and this will always be "the man in the street." Arguments must therefore be crude, clear and forcible, and appeal to emotions and instincts, not the intellect. Truth was unimportant and entirely subordinate to tactics and psychology.

—Joseph Goebbels

Not only was this more propaganda, these were classic disinformation operations which were easily articulated. They're assumed to be true because the credential of "law professor" carries a certain amount of weight. But these are easily discredited as lies, because they are lies that can be proven to be lies.

Today's media is trying to use propaganda, leverage disinformation, and create an "Illusion of Truth" in order to distract the American voting public from the indisputable facts in Round Two.

Are we to ignore the fact that Kamala Harris was born to a Jamaican father with a Jamaican passport and an Indian mother with an Indian passport? Two foreign nationals with passports had a baby in America. By the letter of immigration law, Ms. Harris is the classic dual national. Professor Duggan should know the issue of "natural born citizen" when seeking the office of the president isn't about *residency* but about how (of American citizens) one is born. More disinformation.

It should be obvious to reasonable and rational people that it actually does matter where Ms. Harris' parents were born if their little girl ever wanted to be the President when she grew up. It also matters when they renounced their allegiance to their birth country and became naturalized U.S. citizens. Did either of Ms. Harris' acknowledged foreign parents ever become a naturalized U.S. citizen? Her father, yes. Her mother, no, not ever. This is Obama Part Two, in a dress. Has anyone ever seen Ms. Harris' records? No.

Did Kamala Harris' parents report the blessed birth of their infant to New Delhi and Kingston as required by the laws of their countries, the countries that issued their passports? Or did they ignore their country's laws and simply rejoice in the fact that their daughter was born in America? Let's look at the direct evidence that is in the public domain.

Kamala Harris was born in 1964. Mr. Donald Harris and Ms. Gopalan received a birth certificate from an American hospital, a document attesting to the birth of Kamala Harris. Researchers have determined that the normal path to becoming a naturalized U.S. citizen takes five years. Her father emigrated from Jamaica to America in 1961. Her mother emigrated from India to the U.S. in 1960. At the time and place of Kamala Harris' birth, it appears that Mr. Harris and Ms. Shyamala Gopalan Harris held foreign passports and had entered the United States on student visas.

Several recent reasonable articles suggest *there had not been sufficient time* for either of Kamala's parents to apply for U.S. citizenship, renounce their foreign citizenship, return their passports, and become naturalized

U.S. citizens before the 1964 birth of their daughter. According to his official biography, Kamala's father eventually became a naturalized U.S. citizen. There are no available records to determine if Kamala's mother ever renounced her Indian citizenship or became a naturalized U.S. citizen.

There are records showing that Shyamala Gopalan Harris moved to Canada with Kamala when Kamala was about seven years old. Kamala's mother might have been naturalized as a Canadian citizen, but those records are not available and the vice president will not provide details or documents. Kamala Harris's mother has been deceased since 2009.

Records of presidential candidates with questionable credentials have a disconcerting way of being sealed, and removed from the hands of investigators and the eyes of researchers. Specifically, Democrat candidates. Previous Democrat presidents. Words of wisdom from Barack Obama: seal those records early!

Interesting. Even more interesting is that it is always Democrats with the questionable credentials.

To square the circle on Senator Kamala Harris and her constitutional eligibility to run for the office of the president and later, vice president, Ms. Harris and her staff have refused to answer any questions regarding the citizenship status of her parents when she was born. Maybe the law offices of Perkins Coie have the documents.

Neither Obama nor Harris have been transparent on the issue of their dual nationality. Obama allowed the media to fight his battles on constitutional eligibility on the airwaves and in print. Today the media is flat-out ignoring Kamala Harris'.

Newbusters.org said it best[3], "Every day it becomes more evident that the liberal news media are no longer simply a megaphone for liberals in Washington, New York, and Hollywood. The media are now leading the radical Left and using their platform to push a socialist agenda."

In order to push a socialist agenda a leader is required.

CHAPTER 18
NATURAL BORN CITIZENSHIP: IT'S NOT WHERE YOU ARE BORN, BUT HOW

In January 2016, Congressman Alan Grayson said he would sue Senator Ted Cruz (R-Tex) over his eligibility to be President[1]. Grayson told MSNBC that he would sue over Canadian-born Cruz's natural-born citizen status if the senator ever became the GOP nominee. Why? "Because the Constitution means what it says and says what it means." In February 2016, Presidential Candidate Donald Trump jumped into the fray and said he was "very seriously" thinking about filing a suit to challenge Ted Cruz's eligibility to be President[2]. Senator Cruz' father was a Cuban-born Cuban; his mother was American. "He was born in Canada, lived there for years." Presumably, Mr. Trump's suit would have sought to determine if his competitor was a "natural born citizen" as stipulated by the U.S. Constitution. Congressman Grayson and Mr. Trump's threats of a lawsuit seemed to suggest Senator Cruz's birthplace in Canada would render him ineligible to be President of the United States.

As we have seen, *where* a Presidential candidate was born is not a *de facto* eligibility disqualifier for the Office of President. Doesn't anyone in the media or the Democrat Party do research anymore? Senator John McCain was born to American parents[3] while his father served in the U.S. Navy in Panama. Had he been elected, he would have been the first president born outside the 50 states. Senator Mitt Romney's father was born in Mexico[4], and the elder Romney's eligibility to run for President in 1968 was hardly questioned. George W. Romney was born of American citizens living in a Mormon Church colony in Chihuahua, Mexico.

What is going on here? Contrary to what the Democrats and the media have reported over the last dozen years with respect to the eligibility of the Office of President, it's not always a case of *where* you are born. It is *how* you are born. Any discussion of the Article II *eligibility* requirements for the Office of President during the 2008 election season conveniently ignored any discussion of Barack Obama's eligibility. He was elected President. At this point, does it matter?

During the 2007/8 election cycle, Democrats and the media buttressed Candidate Barack Obama's eligibility to be president with an unrelenting propaganda campaign of repeating the BIG LIE, having been born in Hawaii automatically made Candidate Obama a "natural born citizen." Everyone in the United States knew you had to be a "natural born citizen" to be the President. Not everyone knew to be a "natural born citizen" you had to have parents who were U.S. citizens. The corrupt media ignored the fact that Barack Obama II was a child of a Kenyan national and maintained their narrative. The *Federalist Papers*, the *Naturalization Act of* 1790, and the discussions at the time of the ratification of the U.S. Constitution never qualified a "natural born citizen" by the location where a baby was born, only that they were born of U.S. citizens.

Senator Obama was disqualified to be president for only one reason: he was not born of U.S. citizens.

If anyone had cause to sue over his eligibility it was Senator John McCain. To have the question of what constitutes "natural born citizen" answered once and for all—*resolved*—Senator McCain should have taken Senator Barack Obama to court, to the Supreme Court. *McCain vs Obama.* Some twenty *dozen* distinguished Americans tried to sue President Obama over his eligibility to serve as president but failed; the courts ruled that they had no standing. Only a presidential candidate would have a case to sue another presidential candidate. See *Bush vs. Gore.*

We submit, Barack Obama would not have been able to withstand the court challenge. It would have required unsealing his records during the discovery phase of a trial. Immigration documents. Passports. College applications. It seems being afraid of being called a racist trumped truth, justice, and the American way. McCain folded.

In other words, propaganda works. It turned a war hero who had already endured torture at the hands of an enemy into a shrinking violet, who in his own mind couldn't criticize a black man.

Of the 330-350 million people living in America, only Donald Trump was able to get President Obama and the Democrat Party to interrupt their propaganda and respond to the issue of his eligibility. In response, the White House released a certificate of live birth. What Donald Trump wanted was Barack Obama's *sealed records*. President Obama would never give them up.

What made Barack Hussein Obama II so special to the Democrat Party that they and the media would lie to Americans, and commit crimes that resembled acts of espionage, e.g., forging documents and submitting bogus documents? Was there an *imperative* for Barack Obama to be elected?

We say there are boxes full of evidence that say "yes."

We demonstrated the Democrat Party and the media conducted psychological operations against the American people. They used large scale propaganda on the American voter to elect Barack Obama. Had the Democrat Party and the media ever supplicated themselves like that for any other candidate in memory?

Democrats and the media also refused to engage in any discussion about President Obama's religion. President Obama's father was a Muslim. Isn't a child born of one or two Jewish parents considered a Jewish person? Isn't a child born of one or two Buddhist parents a Buddhist? Isn't a child born of one or two Muslim parents also a Muslim? If a person claims to be a Christian but their official activities help Muslims, domestically and internationally, doesn't that suggest that person is a Muslim? If that same person hides photographs of their associations with Muslims, doesn't that suggest they are Muslim or are sympathetic to Islam? Was Michele Obama's Christianity the camouflage needed for her husband to get elected as a "Christian" and function clandestinely as a Muslim? From a counterterrorism perspective, this looks to be the case. Michelle's Christianity allowed Barack's Mohammedanism.

Who was the Muslim Brotherhood waiting for to establish a secret shadow government within the Government? Who was the Muslim Brotherhood waiting for to establish discreet and secret leadership in government? We think it was Barack Obama hiding behind Michelle. When Barack Obama declared, in front of a throng of thousands, "We are the ones we've been waiting for," was he sending a message? Did he announce that they had infiltrated the U.S. government and gained access to America's secrets?

Many on the Right have tried to make the case using the spirit and intent of his own words from "The Audacity of Hope," that President

Obama would obviously stand with Islam and Muslims "should the political winds shift in an ugly direction[5]." It's hard to defend a man whose daily words and actions can be interpreted as being overly sympathetic to Islam and Muslims to the detriment of America and Americans. Isn't this another way of saying, "If I am ever forced from my operational disguise as a Christian, please know I will always stand with Islam?"

On September 11, 2001, America was attacked by 19 Muslim men of an al-Qaeda affiliate. They hijacked four aircraft and flew three of them into buildings, murdering thousands. Over the past several decades, the vast majority of terrorist attacks against American aviation and America's infrastructure have been perpetrated by one group, men proclaiming to be of the Muslim faith. Counterterrorism specialists know the Muslim faith is not the issue, but *radical Muslims* have used Islam as a shield or camouflage for their murderous operations.

Americans generally do not know that virtually every Islamic country is a U.S. ally (except Iran or Syria). Almost exclusively they buy and fly American fighters and cargo aircraft, buy American commercial jets, their people attend American universities and their military officers attend U.S. flight schools, service academies and war colleges. But the Democrat Party and the media's propaganda is strong in this area, and there are not enough stories of U.S.-Islamic partnership to counter the lies that we are at war with Islam. America is a partner with Islamic nations and like Islamic nations, our allies, we too are at war with their radicals.

Counterterrorism specialists from the CIA and the FBI are in firm agreement, that no matter where the bombers, hijackers, and attackers resided or originated, much of their radicalization took place first in the *madrassas*. They then completed their training in mosques. Islamic nations have a right-wing and a left-wing too, and their lefties fund many radical mosques with fiery imams in their countries and in this country. Those radical mosques, way stations for terrorists and radicals, used to be under surveillance by the FBI. Suspected terrorists or those with suspicious terrorism connections were placed on the terrorist screening database and on no-fly lists[6].

Once the Obama administration moved into the White House it acted to protect radical Muslims in America and their places of worship. Since October 2011, mosques have been off-limits to FBI agents. No more surveillance or undercover sting operations without high-level approval from a special oversight body at the Justice Department dubbed the Sensitive Operations Review Committee.

Finally, in Carol Brown's January 8, 2015 *American Thinker* piece, *Mosques on the Front Lines in the War against America*[7], she noticed, "As the Islamic invasion advances, mosques are proliferating across the United States at breakneck speed. And there appears to be no end[8] in sight. Since 9/11, the number of mosques in America has grown by 75%. The timing of this is no coincidence. Mosques are a symbol of Islamic supremacism. Islam attacks. Then it plants a triumphal mosque on the battlefield. And another. And another. And another. The proliferation of mosques is also a sign of our incomprehensible response (or lack thereof) to the threat of Islam. War has been waged against the United States and what have we done? We have welcomed the enemy with open arms."

FINAL THOUGHTS

Remember what it was like in America on September 11, 2001. Suicidal al-Qaeda murderers had penetrated airport security firewalls, hijacked four jets, and terrorized a nation. Smoke from collapsed buildings in New York City rose continuously for days. Special Operations Command dispatched search and destroy teams to Afghanistan for the illusive Osama bin Laden. The Federal Government nationalized airport screening efforts, created the Department of Homeland Security, and worked to ensure al-Qaeda and the Muslim Brotherhood would not find America asleep at the wheel again.

President Bush spent a great deal of time warning Americans not to overreact or take unlawful actions against Muslims in America. With the 9/11 attacks, Islamic adventurism in America, which had been quietly taking place throughout the country, looked as if it would be set back for several years.

It was the perfect time for the leadership of the Muslim Brotherhood to knock the dust off their *Explanatory Memorandum*. They had a plan to infiltrate and conquer America but the plan cried out for a leader. They had been waiting a very long time for the right person to come to their aid. It couldn't be just anyone.

Counterterrorism specialists saw that he came out of nowhere. He was everything the Muslim Brotherhood had hoped for. With the help of a Christian wife, and attending Chicago's Trinity United Church of Christ, as well as the Democrat Party and a corrupt media he was not only a contender, but with the heavy hand of Nazi-style propaganda, suborned the U.S. Constitution and won an elected office for which he wasn't eligible.

The Muslim Brotherhood's connection with Barack Obama is more than circumstantial. Nation of Islam leader Farrakhan was too extreme and controversial, suggesting an openly Muslim man could not be the leader of the Muslim Brotherhood initiative. A Christian man was out of the question. But hiding behind a Christian wife and declaring your religion was "Unaffiliated" could have been the special disguise needed to infiltrate the Democrat Party. Reportedly "Christian" for the sake of the media and under the concept of *jus sanguinis*, Barack Obama II, the son of a Muslim Kenyan national, was considered Muslim by birth. Pretending to be someone he wasn't and lying for the sake of Islam to gain the upper-hand over an enemy is *taqiya*. President Obama was the one the Muslim Brotherhood had been waiting for after all. Obama leveraged the power of his office to allow the infiltration of Muslims into the United States and the government "until such time as Muslims are powerful enough to progress to violent *jihad* for the final conquest." Left wing propaganda would continue to lionize him as a Christian for things he accomplished for Islam.

The leftist media hid, deflected, and lied about how extensive the Obama Muslim Outreach efforts were in the U.S. government. We stated that President Obama told the NASA Administrator, MajGen Charles Bolden, that his highest priority should be "...to find a way to reach out to the Muslim world[1] and engage much more with dominantly Muslim nations to help them feel good about their historic contribution to science...and math and engineering." The former head of NASA, Michael Griffin, took umbrage with Bolden's statement which he described as "deeply flawed," of the idea that the space exploration agency's priority should be outreach to Muslim countries. He said, "NASA ... represents the best of America. Its purpose is not to inspire Muslims or any other cultural entity." Michael Griffin, who served as NASA administrator during the latter half of the Bush administration, also said that while welcome, Muslim-nation cooperation is not vital for U.S. advancements in space exploration. "There is no technology they have that we need." The former administrator stressed that any criticism should be directed at Obama, not Bolden, since NASA merely carries out policy.

President Obama famously mocked candidate Donald Trump for being a birther[2]. And in his typical arrogant and condescending fashion, he dismissed Trump as having no chance of winning the election. "I continue to believe that Mr. Trump will not be president," Obama said[3]. "And the reason is because I have a lot of faith in the American people." Lost in these events was the conduct of Obama which was anything but presidential.

When Donald Trump was elected President he immediately derailed the freight train that was Obama's Muslim Outreach programs across the federal government. Senator Ted Cruz (R-TX) and Rep. Mario Diaz-Balart (R-FL) introduced a bill to ask the Secretary of State to designate the Muslim Brotherhood as an international terrorist organization[4]. Cruz said, "It's time to call the enemy by its name." And one of the consequences of Mrs. Clinton not getting elected wasn't that there would be no third term for Barack Obama, but that Obama's Muslim Outreach was shut down, and may have set back the Muslim Brotherhood's infiltration and expansion plans for decades. Hillary Clinton's top campaign aide, Huma Abedin, removed boxes from the U.S. State Department, at least one was described as "Muslim Engagement Documents."[5]

They will need a new *Explanatory Memorandum.*

When Donald Trump was elected President, he immediately derailed the freight train that was Obama's Muslim Outreach programs across the federal government. And not only that, President Trump put a stop to the President Obama's scheme to implement government-provided propaganda for the citizens of the United States. Under Executive Order 13707, entitled: *Using Behavioral Science Insights to Better Serve the American People*[6], if that's not an Orwellian title for government controlling the minds of all Americans, we don't what is.

We believe you will understand our position, that Barack Obama was not who he claimed to be and never had any allegiance to America.

The Founders got it right all along. To avoid any split allegiance to another country *or a religion*, candidates seeking the Office of the President need to demonstrate that they are Americans first, that they are born of Americans, that they love this country, and that they will do whatever is necessary to protect and defend the Constitution against all enemies, foreign and domestic.

REFERENCES

Notes from the Authors

1. https://www.thepostemail.com/2012/11/12/the-obama-eligibility-question/
https://www.foxnews.com/politics/kamala-harris-birther-eligibility-conspiracy-theory-dirty-tactics
2. https://www.learning-mind.com/the-illusion-of-truth-manipulation/

Chapter 1 The Hidden Imperative to Amend the U.S. Constitution

1. https://www.congress.gov/bill/94th-congress/house-joint-resolution/33 https://www.congress.gov/bill/95th-congress/house-joint-resolution/38
2. https://www.govtrack.us/congress/bills/108/hjres59
3. https://www.congress.gov/bill/108th-congress/house-joint-resolution/67
4. https://www.congress.gov/bill/108th-congress/senate-bill/2128
5. https://www.congress.gov/bill/108th-congress/house-joint-resolution/104
6. https://www.congress.gov/bill/109th-congress/house-joint-resolution/2
7. https://www.congress.gov/bill/109th-congress/house-joint-resolution/15
8. https://www.congress.gov/bill/109th-congress/house-joint-resolution/42
9. https://www.congress.gov/bill/110th-congress/senate-bill/2678

10. https://www.loc.gov/search/?q=natural%20born%20citizen&fa=digitized:true

Chapter 2 The Natural Born Citizen Clause

1. https://www.americanthinker.com/blog/2021/03/the_washington_post_confessed_to_a_very_big_lie.html
2. https://en.wikipedia.org/wiki/Natural-born-citizen_clause
3. https://www.sfgate.com/politics/article/Amend-for-Arnold-campaign-launched-Web-site-2635267.php
4. https://www.msn.com/en-us/news/politics/cnn-director-shown-on-undercover-video-boasting-about-removing-trump-from-office-and-admitting-to-spreading-propaganda/ar-BB1fCA7W
5. https://www.breitbart.com/the-media/2021/05/28/this-is-dncnn-breaking-the-news-reveals-deep-ties-between-cnn-democrat-power-players/
6. https://en.wikipedia.org/wiki/Article_Two_of_the_United_States_Constitution
7. No, Arnold Schwarzenegger Can't Be President—And This Is Dumb – ThinkProgress https://archive.thinkprogress.org/no-arnold-schwarzenegger-cant-be-president-and-this-is-dumb-5d2bc64a21f2/
8. https://en.wikipedia.org/wiki/The_Law_of_Nations
9. https://www.loc.gov/law/help/statutes-at-large/1st-congress/c1.pdf
10. https://oll.libertyfund.org/title/farrand-the-records-of-the-federal-convention-of-1787-vol-1#preview
11. http://oll-resources.s3.amazonaws.com/titles/1787/0544-03_Bk.pdf
12. https://avalon.law.yale.edu/18th_century/fed68.asp
13. Why Is Obama's Middle Name Taboo? - TIME http://content.time.com/time/politics/article/0,8599,1718255,00.html

14. Candidate Obama does not cover his heart during the National Anthem: https://www.youtube.com/watch?app=desktop&v=hU9iCANi02o&feature=youtu.be
15. Candidate Obama does not cover his heart during the National Anthem: https://www.youtube.com/watch?app=desktop&v=hU9iCANi02o&feature=youtu.be https://humanevents.com/2010/08/19/obama-muslim-call-to-prayer-one-of-the-prettiest-sounds-on-earth/
16. https://en.wikipedia.org/wiki/Taqiya
17. https://abcnews.go.com/blogs/politics/2012/05/obama-and-his-pot-smoking-choom-gang
18. https://stephanieavery.wordpress.com/2009/09/24/i-thought-bill-ayers-was-just-a-guy-in-the-neighborhood/

Chapter 3 America's Media and their Unholy Relationship with the Democrat Party

1. https://pjmedia.com/news-and-politics/tyler-o-neil/2021/04/13/watch-cnn-director-admits-network-ran-propaganda-to-get-trump-voted-out-n1439680
2. https://thefederalist.com/2021/05/12/behind-the-curtain-how-the-new-york-times-manufactures-lies-for-democrats-to-attack-their-opponents/
3. https://www.cnn.com/2021/04/30/politics/rudy-giuliani-russia-influence-campaign/index.html
4. https://www.learning-mind.com/the-illusion-of-truth-manipulation/
5. https://www.politifact.com/factchecks/2019/jan/22/jacob-wohl/yes-kamala-harris-eligible-run-president/
6. https://canadafreepress.com/article/the-theory-is-now-a-conspiracy-and-facts-dont-lie
7. http://www.cnn.com/2003/WORLD/meast/03/31/sprj.irq.geraldo/

Chapter 4 Why the Media Wouldn't Conduct a Study

1. https://www.amazon.com/Shariah-America-Exercise-Competitive-Analysis/dp/098229476X/ref=sr_1_1?dchild=1&keywords=SHARIA%3A+The+Threat+to+America&qid=1614374759&sr=8-1
2. https://www.amazon.com/Explanatory-Memorandum-Archives-Brotherhood-Security/dp/0982294719/ref=sr_1_1?dchild=1&keywords=An+Explanatory+Memorandum&qid=1614374908&sr=8-1

Chapter 5 What the Law Reviews Actually Reveal

1. https://digitalcommons.law.umaryland.edu/cgi/viewcontent.cgi?article=2068&context=mlr
2. https://en.wikipedia.org/wiki/Jus_soli
3. https://en.wikipedia.org/wiki/Nationality
4. https://en.wikipedia.org/wiki/Jus_sanguinis
5. https://en.wikipedia.org/wiki/Citizenship
6. https://core.ac.uk/reader/270182092
7. https://scholarship.law.georgetown.edu/cgi/viewcontent.cgi?article=1846&context=facpub
8. https://scholarship.law.umn.edu/cgi/viewcontent.cgi?article=1941&context=concomm
9. https://scholarship.law.umn.edu/cgi/viewcontent.cgi?article=1463&context=concomm
10. https://repository.law.umich.edu/cgi/viewcontent.cgi?article=1089&context=mlr_fi
11. https://digitalcommons.law.yale.edu/cgi/viewcontent.cgi?article=7137&context=ylj
12. https://repository.law.umich.edu/cgi/viewcontent.cgi?article=1089&context=mlr_fi
13. https://www.congress.gov/bill/110th-congress/senate-resolution/511/text
14. http://blogs.gonzaga.edu/gulawreview/files/2011/01/Lohman1.pdf

Chapter 6 What the Founders Actually Said; Why the Media had to use propaganda

1. https://thenationalpulse.com/breaking/biden-eo-oath-of-allegiance/
2. https://www.uscis.gov/citizenship/learn-about-citizenship/the-naturalization-interview-and-test/naturalization-oath-of-allegiance-to-the-united-states-of-america
3. https://thenationalpulse.com/breaking/biden-eo-oath-of-allegiance/
4. http://blogs.gonzaga.edu/gulawreview/files/2011/01/Lohman1.pdf
5. https://www.foxnews.com/politics/kamala-harris-birther-eligibility-conspiracy-theory-dirty-tactics

Chapter 7 Citizenship and Allegiance

1. https://brill.com/view/book/edcoll/9789004417342/BP000008.xml?language=en
2. https://travel.state.gov/content/travel/en/legal/travel-legal-considerations/Advice-about-Possible-Loss-of-US-Nationality-Dual-Nationality/Dual-Nationality.html
3. https://travel.state.gov/content/travel/en/international-travel/before-you-go/travelers-with-special-considerations/Dual-Nationality-Travelers.html http://islam101.com/dawah/newBorn.htm
4. From Figure IN2 of Nick Chase's American Thinker article: https://www.americanthinker.com/articles/2012/07/were_ann_dunham_and_barack_obama_really_married.html
5. https://www.zawaj.com/divorce-in-islam-by-islamonline/
6. https://en.wikipedia.org/wiki/Natural-born-citizen_clause
7. https://en.wikipedia.org/wiki/Presidential_Succession_Act
8. https://en.wikipedia.org/wiki/Constitution_of_Mexico

Chapter 8 The Stuff We're Not Supposed to Talk About

1. https://politicrossing.com/breaking-cnn-executive-admits-propaganda-to-defeat-trump/
2. http://historynewsnetwork.org/article/162096
3. http://www.psywarrior.com/9thPOBnA.html
4. https://welovetrump.com/2020/05/23/msnbcs-mika-brzezinski-haunted-by-video-saying-its-our-job-to-control-exactly-what-people-think/
5. https://www.npr.org/2020/01/22/798561799/architect-of-cias-torture-program-says-it-went-too-far#:~:text=Alleged%20Sept.%2011%20mastermind%20Khalid%20Sheikh%20Mohammed%20%28far,Air%20Force%20psychologist%20James%20Mitchell%2C%20takes%20the%20stand.

Chapter 9 Republican Presidential Nominee Senator John McCain

1. https://en.wikipedia.org/wiki/John_McCain
2. https://repository.law.umich.edu/cgi/viewcontent.cgi?article=1089&context=mlr_fi
3. http://journaloflaw.us/1%20Pub.%20L.%20Misc./2-2/JoL2-3,%20PLM2-2,%20Tribe%20and%20Olson.pdf
4. https://www.dhs.gov/immigration-statistics/nonimmigrant/NonimmigrantCOA
5. Directory of Visa Categories (state.gov) https://travel.state.gov/content/travel/en/us-visas/visa-information-resources/all-visa-categories.html

Chapter 10 Democrat Presidential Nominee Senator Barack Obama II

1. https://en.wikipedia.org/wiki/Barack_Obama
2. https://travel.state.gov/content/travel/en/legal/travel-legal-considerations/us-citizenship.html
3. https://klrc.go.ke/index.php/constitution-of-kenya/109-chapter-three-citizenship/180-14-citizenship-by-birth

4. https://travel.state.gov/content/travel/en/legal/travel-legal-considerations/Advice-about-Possible-Loss-of-US-Nationality-Dual-Nationality/Dual-Nationality.html
5. Multiple citizenship - Wikipedia https://en.wikipedia.org/wiki/Multiple_citizenship
6. https://klrc.go.ke/index.php/constitution-of-kenya/109-chapter-three-citizenship/182-16-dual-citizenship
7. https://kenyaembassydc.org/download/birth-certificate-kenyan-born-abroad-form-bda-1/
8. Unnatural Born Citizens and Acting Presidents (umn.edu) https://scholarship.law.umn.edu/cgi/viewcontent.cgi?article=1463&context=concomm
9. Obama: "My Muslim Faith" video https://www.youtube.com/watch?reload=9&app=desktop&v=XKGdkqfBICw https://www.foxnews.com/politics/kamala-harris-birther-eligibility-conspiracy-theory-dirty-tactics
10. BROKEN RECORD: Brian Stelter Puts On Carl Bernstein to Call Trump a Domestic War Criminal | Newsbusters https://www.newsbusters.org/blogs/nb/tim-graham/2021/07/25/broken-record-brian-stelter-puts-carl-bernstein-call-trump-domestic

Chapter 11 If it's not Brainwashing, Then What Is It?

1. https://www.amazon.com/Dark-Psychology-Manipulation-Techniques-Brainwashing/dp/B08M8Y5G36/ref=sr_1_4?dchild=1&keywords=Dark+Psychology+and+Manipulation&qid=1626415003&s=books&sr=1-4
2. https://www.amazon.com/Manchurian-Candidate-Richard-Condon-ebook/dp/B087N6SH3H/ref=sr_1_1_sspa?dchild=1&keywords=The+Manchurian+Candidate&qid=1618176608&s=books&sr=1-1-spons&psc=1&spLa=ZW5jcnlwdGVkUXVhbGlmaWVyPUEzMVY2NjBXRlJVNUgmZW5jcnlwdGVkSWQ9QTA4MDEyODE0RzQ0

OUhIRDNMRDAmZW5jcnlwdGVkQWRJZD1BMDM2MjAxNTFCUloyTUhTMk9LVEUmd2lkZ2V0TmFtZT1zcF9hdGYmYWN0aW9uPWNsaWNrUmVkaXJlY3QmZG9Ob3RMb2dDbGljaz10cnVl
3. https://en.wikipedia.org/wiki/Project_ARTICHOKE
4. https://publicintelligence.net/cia-bluebird/
5. https://en.wikipedia.org/wiki/Operation_Mockingbird
6. http://www.danwismar.com/uploads/Bernstein%20-%20CIA%20and%20Media.htm#:~:text=The%20CIA%20and%20the%20Media%20by%20Carl%20Bernstein,so%20by%20the%20newspapers%20that%20printed%20his%20column.

Chapter 12 Domestic Enemies Require their own Ministry of Propaganda

1. House Un-American Activities Committee - Wikipedia https://en.wikipedia.org/wiki/House_Un-American_Activities_Committee
2. https://en.wikipedia.org/wiki/Leni_Riefenstahl
3. https://www.msn.com/en-us/news/politics/cnn-technical-director-admits-the-network-was-pushing-propaganda-with-fake-stories/ar-BB1fCgUj https://thefederalist.com/2021/05/12/behind-the-curtain-how-the-new-york-times-manufactures-lies-for-democrats-to-attack-their-opponents/
4. Nation of Islam - Wikipedia https://en.wikipedia.org/wiki/Nation_of_Islam
5. https://www.tradeschool.com/blog/barack-obamas-gpa-and-college-records/ https://religiopoliticaltalk.com/trinity-united-church-of-christs-akiba-bookstore/ https://gnet-research.org/2021/03/08/dars-and-madrassas-remnants-of-a-lost-pedagogy-that-has-advanced-onto-the-cyber-realm/

Chapter 13 Barack Obama, Senior

1. https://travel.state.gov/content/travel/en/us-visas/study/student-visa.html

2. https://www.cbp.gov/travel/international-visitors
3. From Figure IN2 of Nick Chase's American Thinker article: https://www.americanthinker.com/articles/2012/07/were_ann_dunham_and_barack_obama_really_married.html
4. https://www.dhs.gov/immigration-statistics/nonimmigrant/NonimmigrantCOA
5. https://travel.state.gov/content/travel/en/us-visas/study/student-visa.html
6. From Figure IN1 of Nick Chase's American Thinker article: https://www.americanthinker.com/articles/2012/07/were_ann_dunham_and_barack_obama_really_married.html
7. https://www.politifact.com/factchecks/2019/jan/22/jacob-wohl/yes-kamala-harris-eligible-run-president/
8. https://www.louderwithcrowder.com/mika-slips-job-tell-think
9. https://www.newsbusters.org/blogs/nb/scott-whitlock/2019/07/16/50-years-shame-how-journalists-protected-ted-kennedy-after

Chapter 14 When Theory Becomes a Conspiracy

1. https://www.newsbusters.org/blogs/nb/scott-whitlock/2019/07/16/50-years-shame-how-journalists-protected-ted-kennedy-after
2. https://www.israelnationalnews.com/Blogs/Message.aspx/3074
3. https://www.israelnationalnews.com/Blogs/Message.aspx/3074
4. https://www.israelnationalnews.com/Blogs/Message.aspx/3074
5. https://www.mcclatchydc.com/news/politics-government/election/article102354777.html
6. https://www.wnd.com/2009/08/107524/
7. https://www.today.com/id/42469703/ns/today-today_news/t/trump-i-have-real-doubts-obama-was-born-us/#.V9w1HfkrK03

8. https://www.cnn.com/2017/11/28/politics/donald-trump-barack-obama-birth-certificate-nyt/index.html
9. https://www.washingtonpost.com/news/post-politics/wp/2016/09/16/trump-said-hed-give-away-5-million-or-maybe-50-million-for-proof-obama-was-born-in-the-u-s-will-he-pay-it/
10. https://www.motherjones.com/politics/2011/05/trump-birth-certificate-jerome-corsi/
11. http://www.orlytaitzesq.com/obamas-campaign-paid-over-5-million-to-perkins-coie-to-keep-his-ids-sealed-i-wonder-if-it-included-a-pay-to-siddharth-velamoor-and-some-clerks-and-court-reporters/
12. https://12160.info/forum/topics/why-did-obama-barry-soetoro-pay-5-million-to-seal-all-his-records https://finance.yahoo.com/news/donald-trump-tax-audited-12-years-in-a-row-161055545.html
13. https://spectator.org/john-brennans-president-remembering-comrade-gus-hall/
14. https://www.newsbusters.org/blogs/nb/scott-whitlock/2019/07/16/50-years-shame-how-journalists-protected-ted-kennedy-after

Chapter 15 The Explanatory Memorandum and a Curious Coincidence

1. https://www.amazon.com/Shariah-America-Exercise-Competitive-Analysis/dp/098229476X/ref=sr_1_1?dchild=1&keywords=SHARIA%3A+The+Threat+to+America&qid=1614374759&sr=8-1
2. https://www.amazon.com/Explanatory-Memorandum-Archives-Brotherhood-Security/dp/0982294719/ref=sr_1_1?dchild=1&keywords=An+Explanatory+Memorandum&qid=1614374908&sr=8-1
3. https://avalon.law.yale.edu/18th_century/fed68.asp

4. https://centerforsecuritypolicy.org/an-explanatory-memorandum-from-the-archives-of-the-muslim-brotherhood-in-america/
5. https://rationalwiki.org/wiki/Explanatory_Memorandum
6. https://www.americanthinker.com/articles/2016/11/barry_shariaseed_and_the_muslim_brotherhood_tree.html
7. https://www.washingtontimes.com/news/2012/sep/11/obama-my-muslim-faith/
8. https://www.brainyquote.com/quotes/barack_obama_409128#:~:text=We%20are%20the%20ones%20we%27ve%20been%20waiting%20for.,a%20gift.%20That%27s%20why%20it%27s%20called%20the%20present.
https://humanevents.com/2010/08/19/obama-muslim-call-to-prayer-one-of-the-prettiest-sounds-on-earth/\
9. Washington Apple Commission (bestapples.com) http://bestapples.com/resources-teachers-corner/johnny-appleseed/ http://shariahthethreat.org/a-short-course-1-what-is-shariah/a-short-course-14-the-muslim-brotherhood%E2%80%99s-strategic-plan/
http://shariahthethreat.org/a-short-course-1-what-is-shariah/a-short-course-3-civilization-jihad/
http://shariahthethreat.org/a-short-course-1-what-is-shariah/a-short-course-14-the-muslim-brotherhood%E2%80%99s-strategic-plan/
10. *Phases of the World Underground Movement Plan* http://shariahthethreat.org/a-short-course-1-what-is-shariah/a-short-course-14-the-muslim-brotherhood%E2%80%99s-strategic-plan/
11. WikiLeaks Report: Obama Admin Discriminated Against Arab Christians for Top Jobs | BWCentral https://bwcentral.org/2016/10/wikileaks-report-obama-admin-discriminated-against-arab-christians-for-top-jobs/
12. NASA's Muslim Outreach | RealClearPolitics https://www.realclearpolitics.com/articles/2010/07/07/nasas_muslim_outreach_106214.html

13. http://www.whitehouse.gov/blog/NewBeginning/transcripts
14. http://www.investors.com/NewsAndAnalysis/Article.aspx?id=577509&p=2
15. Shock claim: Obama picks Muslim for CIA chief (wnd.com) https://www.wnd.com/2013/02/shock-claim-obama-picks-muslim-for-cia-chief/
16. Huma Abedin worked at Muslim journal that opposed women's rights (nypost.com) https://nypost.com/2016/08/21/huma-abedin-worked-at-a-radical-muslim-journal-for-10-years/
17. Daddy's Issues (freebeacon.com) https://freebeacon.com/issues/weiner-father-law-exposed/
18. http://shariahthethreat.org/a-short-course-1-what-is-shariah/a-short-course-5-taqiyya/
19. https://www.dailymail.co.uk/news/article-5314421/Journalist-reveals-photo-Obama-Louis-Farrakhan.html
20. https://religiopoliticaltalk.com/trinity-united-church-of-christs-akiba-bookstore/ https://freebeacon.com/national-security/muslim-brotherhood-leader-meets-obama-in-white-house/ http://hurryupharry.net/
21. Muslim Brotherhood Leader Meets Obama in White House (freebeacon.com) https://freebeacon.com/national-security/muslim-brotherhood-leader-meets-obama-in-white-house/
22. https://www.brainyquote.com/quotes/barack_obama_409128#:~:text=We%20are%20the%20ones%20we%27ve%20been%20waiting%20for.,a%20gift.%20That%27s%20why%20it%27s%20called%20the%20present.

Chapter 16 When Donald Trump and Barack Obama's Paths Crossed

1. Obama Born In Kenya? His Grandmother Says Yes. - Israel National News

https://www.israelnationalnews.com/Blogs/Message.aspx/3074

2. Obama Born In Kenya? His Grandmother Says Yes. - Israel National News https://www.israelnationalnews.com/Blogs/Message.aspx/3074
3. 2 Clinton supporters in '08 reportedly shared Obama 'birther' story | McClatchy Washington Bureau (mcclatchydc.com) https://www.mcclatchydc.com/news/politics-government/election/article102354777.html
4. Did Obama's grandmother say he was born in Kenya? (wnd.com) https://www.wnd.com/2009/08/107524/
5. https://www.abdn.ac.uk/news/10040/
6. https://www.today.com/id/42469703/ns/today-today_news/t/trump-i-have-real-doubts-obama-was-born-us/#.V9w1HfkrK03
7. Report: Trump continues to question Obama's birth certificate | CNN https://www.cnn.com/2017/11/28/politics/donald-trump-barack-obama-birth-certificate-nyt/index.html
8. Trump said he'd give away $5 million — or maybe $50 million — for proof Obama was born in the U.S. Will he pay it? - The Washington Post
9. https://www.washingtonpost.com/news/post-politics/wp/2016/09/16/trump-said-hed-give-away-5-million-or-maybe-50-million-for-proof-obama-was-born-in-the-u-s-will-he-pay-it/
10. Donald Trump says he'll donate $5 million to charity if Obama releases college, passport records (video) - al.com https://www.al.com/tuscaloosa/2012/10/donald_trump_says_hell_donate.html
11. Why did Obama/Barry Soetoro Pay $5 Million to Seal ALL His Records - 12160 Social Network https://12160.info/forum/topics/why-did-obama-barry-soetoro-pay-5-million-to-seal-all-his-records

12. Trump: Birther Jerome Corsi Got it Wrong – Mother Jones https://www.motherjones.com/politics/2011/05/trump-birth-certificate-jerome-corsi/
13. Obama's campaign paid over 5 million to Perkins Coie to keep his IDs sealed, I wonder if it included a pay to Siddharth Velamoor and some clerks and court reporters? : OrlyTaitzEsq.com http://www.orlytaitzesq.com/obamas-campaign-paid-over-5-million-to-perkins-coie-to-keep-his-ids-sealed-i-wonder-if-it-included-a-pay-to-siddharth-velamoor-and-some-clerks-and-court-reporters/
14. Why did Obama/Barry Soetoro Pay $5 Million to Seal ALL His Records - 12160 Social Network https://12160.info/forum/topics/why-did-obama-barry-soetoro-pay-5-million-to-seal-all-his-records
15. DNC, Clinton campaign paid for research that resulted in Trump dossier: Report - CBS News https://www.cbsnews.com/news/dnc-clinton-campaign-paid-for-research-in-trump-dossier-report/
16. Why would Donald Trump get audited 12 years in a row? (yahoo.com) https://finance.yahoo.com/news/donald-trump-tax-audited-12-years-in-a-row-161055545.html
17. John Brennan's President... Remembering Comrade Gus Hall | The American Spectator | USA News and Politics https://spectator.org/john-brennans-president-remembering-comrade-gus-hall/

Chapter 17 It Happened Again with Senator Kamala Harris

1. https://defconnews.com/2019/07/14/check-out-what-liberal-douche-thinks-ar-15-stands-for/
2. https://www.politifact.com/factchecks/2019/jan/22/jacob-wohl/yes-kamala-harris-eligible-run-president/
3. https://www.newsbusters.org/blogs/nb/scott-whitlock/2019/07/16/50-years-shame-how-journalists-protected-ted-kennedy-after

Chapter 18 Natural Born Citizen: It's not Where You are Born but How

1. Alan Grayson Explains Why He'll Sue Ted Cruz Over Presidential Eligibility – PJ Media https://pjmedia.com/election/bridget-johnson/2016/01/15/alan-grayson-explains-why-hell-sue-ted-cruz-over-presidential-eligibility-n43567
2. Donald Trump 'seriously thinking' about suing Ted Cruz | CNN https://www.cnn.com/2016/02/16/politics/donald-trump-ted-cruz-lawsuit-threat/
3. PolitiFact | Was McCain born in the USA? https://www.politifact.com/article/2008/may/12/born-usa/
4. How Mitt Romney's Mexican-Born Father Was Eligible to be President - ABC News (go.com) https://abcnews.go.com/blogs/politics/2012/01/how-mitt-romneys-mexican-born-father-was-eligible-to-be-president/
5. Obama's 'Dreams of My Father' - FactCheck.org https://www.factcheck.org/2008/06/obamas-dreams-of-my-father/
6. DHS/ALL/PIA-027 Watchlist Service | Homeland Security https://www.dhs.gov/publication/dhs-all-pia-027c-watchlist-service-update
7. Mosques on the front lines in the war against America (americanthinker.com)https://www.americanthinker.com/articles/2015/01/mosques_on_the_front_lines_in_the_war_against_america.html
8. List of mosques in the United States - Wikipedia https://en.wikipedia.org/wiki/List_of_mosques_in_the_United_States

Final Thoughts

1. Former NASA Director Says Muslim Outreach Push 'Deeply Flawed' | Fox News

https://www.foxnews.com/politics/former-nasa-director-says-muslim-outreach-push-deeply-flawed

2. Obama mocks Trump at White House Correspondents' Dinner (nypost.com) https://nypost.com/2011/05/01/obama-mocks-trump-at-white-house-correspondents-dinner/
3. FLASHBACK: Obama Mocks Trump, Says He'll Never Be President (thepoliticalinsider.com) https://thepoliticalinsider.com/obama-trump-mocks-says-never-president/
4. Ted Cruz Introduces Bill To Designate Muslim Brotherhood As Terrorist Organization by Christine Rousselle (townhall.com) https://townhall.com/tipsheet/christinerousselle/2017/01/11/ted-cruz-introduces-bill-to-designate-muslim-brotherhood-as-terrorist-organization-n2269714
5. State Allowed Huma to Remove Records, Including "Muslim Engagement Documents" - www.independentsentinel.com https://www.independentsentinel.com/state-allowed-huma-to-remove-records-including-muslim-engagement-documents/
6. Executive Order -- Using Behavioral Science Insights to Better Serve the American People | whitehouse.gov (archives.gov) https://obamawhitehouse.archives.gov/the-press-office/2015/09/15/executive-order-using-behavioral-science-insights-better-serve-american

EXHIBITS

1. PRESIDENTS AND CITIZENSHIP Opinion letter by Laurence H. Tribe and Theodore Olson

PRESIDENTS AND CITIZENSHIP

Opinion letter by Laurence H. Tribe and Theodore B. Olson

March 19, 2008

We have analyzed whether Senator John McCain is eligible for the U.S. Presidency, in light of the requirement under Article II of the U.S. Constitution that only "natural born Citizen[s] . . . shall be eligible to the Office of President." U.S. Const. art. II, § 1, cl. 5. We conclude that Senator McCain is a "natural born Citizen" by virtue of his birth in 1936 to U.S. citizen parents who were serving their country on a U.S. military base in the Panama Canal Zone. The circumstances of Senator McCain's birth satisfy the original meaning and intent of the Natural Born Citizen Clause, as confirmed by subsequent legal precedent and historical practice.

The Constitution does not define the meaning of "natural born Citizen." The U.S. Supreme Court gives meaning to terms that are not expressly defined in the Constitution by looking to the context in which those terms are used; to statutes enacted by the First Congress, *Marsh v. Chambers*, 463 U.S. 783, 790-91 (1983); and to the common law at the time of the Founding. *United States v. Wong Kim Ark*, 169 U.S. 649, 655 (1898). These sources all confirm that the phrase "natural born" includes both birth abroad to parents who were citizens, and birth within a nation's territory and allegiance. Thus, regardless of the sovereign status of the Panama Canal Zone at the time of Senator McCain's birth, he is a "natural born" citizen because he was born to parents who were U.S. citizens.

Congress has recognized in successive federal statutes since the Nation's Founding that children born abroad to U.S. citizens are themselves U.S. citizens. 8 U.S.C. § 1401(c); *see also* Act of May 24, 1934, Pub. L. No. 73-250, § 1, 48 Stat. 797, 797. Indeed, the statute that the First Congress enacted on this subject not only established that such children are U.S. citizens, but also expressly referred to them as "natural born citizens." Act of Mar. 26, 1790, ch. 3, § 1, 1 Stat. 103, 104.

TRIBE AND OLSON OPINION LETTER, MAR. 19, 2008

Senator McCain's status as a "natural born" citizen by virtue of his birth to U.S. citizen parents is consistent with British statutes in force when the Constitution was drafted, which undoubtedly informed the Framers' understanding of the Natural Born Citizen Clause. Those statutes provided, for example, that children born abroad to parents who were "natural-born Subjects" were also "natural-born Subjects . . . to all Intents, Constructions and Purposes whatsoever." British Nationality Act, 1730, 4 Geo. 2, c. 21. The Frames substituted the word "citizen" for "subject" to reflect the shift from monarch to democracy, but the Supreme Court has recognized that the two terms are otherwise identical. *See e.g.*, *Hennessy v. Richardson Drug Co.*, 189 U.S. 25, 34-35 (1903). Thus, the First Congress's statutory recognition that persons born abroad to U.S. citizens were "natural born" citizens fully conformed to British tradition, whereby citizenship conferred by statute based on the circumstances of one's *birth* made one *natural born*.

There is a second and independent basis for concluding that Senator McCain is a "natural born" citizen within the meaning of the Constitution. If the Panama Canal Zone was sovereign U.S. territory at the time of Senator McCain's birth, then that fact alone would make him a "natural born" citizen under the well-established principle that "natural born" citizenship includes birth within the territory and allegiance of the United States. *See, e.g.*, *Wong Kim Ark*, 169 U.S. at 655-66. The Fourteenth Amendment expressly enshrines this connection between birthplace and citizenship in the text of the Constitution. U.S. Const. amend. XIV, § 1 ("All persons *born* or naturalized *in the United States*, and subject to the jurisdiction thereof, are citizens of the United States . . . .") (emphases added). Premising "natural born" citizenship on the character of the territory in which one is born is rooted in the common-law understanding that persons born within the British kingdom and under loyalty to the British Crown – including most of the Framers themselves, who were born in the American colonies – were deemed "natural born subjects." *See, e.g.*, 1 William Blackstone, *Commentaries on the Laws of England* 354 (Legal Classics Library 1983) (1765) ("Natural-born subjects are such as are born within the dominions of the crown of

England, that is, within the ligeance, or as it is generally called, the allegiance of the king . . . .").

There is substantial legal support for the proposition that the Panama Canal Zone was indeed sovereign U.S. territory when Senator McCain was born there in 1936. The U.S. Supreme Court has explained that, "[f]rom 1904 to 1979, the United States exercised sovereignty over the Panama Canal and the surrounding 10-mile-wide Panama Canal Zone." *O'Connor v. United States*, 479 U.S. 27, 28 (1986). Congress and the executive branch similarly suggested that the Canal Zone was subject to the sovereignty of the United States. *See, e.g.*, *The President – Government of the Canal Zone*, 26 Op. Att'y Gen. 113, 116 (1907) (recognizing that the 1904 treaty between the United States and Panama "imposed upon the United States the obligations as well as the powers of a sovereign within the [Canal Zone]"); Panama Canal Act of 1912, Pub. L. No. 62-337, § 1, 37 Stat. 560, 560 (recognizing that "the use, occupancy, or control" of the Canal Zone had been "granted to the United States by the treaty between the United States and the Republic of Panama"). Thus, although Senator McCain was not born within a State, there is a significant body of legal authority indicating that he was nevertheless born within the sovereign territory of the United States.

Historical practice confirms that birth on soil that is under the sovereignty of the United States, but not within a State, satisfies the Natural Born Citizen Clause. For example, Vice President Charles Curtis was born in the territory of Kansas on January 25, 1860 – one year before Kansas became a State. Because the Twelfth Amendment requires that Vice Presidents possess the same qualifications as Presidents, the service of Vice President Curtis verifies that the phrase "natural born Citizen" includes birth outside of any State but within U.S. territory. Similarly, Senator Barry Goldwater was born in Arizona before its statehood, yet attained the Republican Party's presidential nomination in 1964. And Senator Barack Obama was born in Hawaii on August 4, 1961 – not long after its admission to the Union on August 21, 1959. We find it inconceivable that Senator Obama would have been ineligible for the Presidency had he been born two years earlier.

Senator McCain's candidacy for the Presidency is consistent not only with the accepted meaning of "natural born Citizen," but also with the Framers' intentions when adopting that language. The Natural Born Citizen Clause was added to the Constitution shortly after John Jay sent a letter to George Washington expressing concern about "Foreigners" attaining the position of Commander in Chief. 3 Max Farrand, *The Records of the Federal Convention of 1787*, at 61 (1911). It goes without saying that the Framers did not intend to exclude a person from the office of the President simply because he or she was born to U.S. citizens serving in the U.S. military outside of the continental United States; Senator McCain is certainly not the hypothetical "Foreigner" who John Jay and George Washington were concerned might usurp the role of Commander in Chief.

Therefore, based on the original meaning of the Constitution, the Framers' intentions, and subsequent legal and historical precedent, Senator McCain's birth to parents who were U.S. citizens, serving on a U.S. military base in the Panama Canal Zone in 1936, makes him a "natural born Citizen" within the meaning of the Constitution.

Laurence H. Tribe   Theodore B. Olson

ACKNOWLEDGEMENTS

A special “THANK YOU to our editors for editing this manuscript.

Any errors found in this book are our responsibility and not the responsibility of the publisher.

The best cover design person in the business must be Dave King. We believe the evidence once again shows him to be King of the Hill.

To Reagan Rothe: There’s a line from *Casablanca*, from Victor Laszlo: *Welcome back to the fight. This time I know our side will win.*

NOTE FROM THE AUTHOR

Word-of-mouth is crucial for any author to succeed. If you enjoyed *The Grand Illusion*, please leave a review online—anywhere you are able. Even if it's just a sentence or two. It would make all the difference and would be very much appreciated.

Thanks!
Laszlo Forseti

www.ingramcontent.com/pod-product-compliance
Lightning Source LLC
Chambersburg PA
CBHW060321030426
42336CB00011B/1146

* 9 7 8 1 6 8 4 3 3 9 3 9 6 *